Teaching Notes on Piano Examination Pieces 2003–2004

Grades 1–7

GW00690887

5-95

CLARA TAYLOR

FRAM FRSA LRAM

Chief Examiner of
The Associated Board of the Royal Schools of Music

ANTHONY WILLIAMS

MMus DipRAM GRSM LRAM

Head of Keyboard and Assistant Director of Music at Radley College

Teaching Notes on Piano Examination Pieces 2003–2004

Grades 1–7

The Associated Board of the Royal Schools of Music

First published in 2002 by
The Associated Board of the Royal Schools of Music (Publishing) Limited
24 Portland Place, London W1B 1LU, United Kingdom

© 2002 by The Associated Board of the Royal Schools of Music

ISBN 1 86096 272 6

AB 2834

All rights reserved. No part of this publication may be reproduced,
stored in a retrieval system, or transmitted in any form or by any
means, electronic, mechanical, photocopying, recording, or otherwise,
without the prior permission of the copyright owner.

A CIP catalogue for this book is available from The British Library.

Typeset by Hope Services (Abingdon) Ltd
Printed in England by Halstan & Co. Ltd, Amersham, Bucks

CONTENTS

Introduction   1

Grade 1   5

Grade 2   16

Grade 3   27

Grade 4   40

Grade 5   54

Grade 6   68

Grade 7   84

INTRODUCTION

The right repertoire is invaluable and the introduction to a new piece is a crucial moment. If the teacher can find a 'way in' to the music – perhaps an imaginative idea, or some words that fit the melody, or a storyline – the pupil will have far more enthusiasm and be able to overcome problem passages with more determination. In these commentaries, Anthony and I have given high priority to suggesting ways to catch a pupil's interest. We hope our ideas for a really polished performance will inspire greater efforts, even though most pupils come into a healthy pass category in their results, with 117 being the overall average mark. Sometimes there is too limited an ability to achieve the higher levels of merit and distinction, but the important thing is that each candidate has lifted his or her standard as a result of the preparation and motivation that an exam brings.

The day-to-day reality of the piano lesson comes strongly to mind when writing these commentaries. It is easy mentally to hear the usual mistakes, wrong rhythms and co-ordination difficulties that will be brought to the lesson for the teacher to solve. This is normal life with normal pupils. Only a tiny minority races through the grades, gaining distinction with comparatively little effort. For most pupils, learning the piano will be one of their most rewarding and enriching experiences, and one that will stay with them forever. The teacher's responsibility is great – too much praise and the pupil will instinctively suspect the truth is not being told, but too little encouragement and the pupil's confidence is damaged, along with his or her desire to continue.

The wide choice of repertoire for every grade gives the opportunity to match the pieces to the pupil. Sometimes you might choose a style that immediately suits, and at other times you might take a more medicinal approach in order to tackle shortcomings. From the lists there are obvious winners, which will appear many times in the exams, but do also explore the alternative pieces not published in the graded volumes. There are some delights to be found that may just be the answer for some pupils.

From Grade 1 to Grade 8 the three lists have more in common than you might expect. List A contains the technically demanding repertoire, List B the more warmly expressive pieces, and List C has a tremendous variety of styles, often with some jazzy rhythms. Despite the enormous difference in standards between Grade 1 and Grade 8, candidates' strengths and weaknesses tend to follow predictable paths in each list. I believe it will be helpful, therefore, to consider the three lists in more detail.

LIST A

In List A, definition of fingerwork, clarity of articulation and control of co-ordination are necessary, as fluency increases through the grades. These technical challenges, especially runs and ornaments, can upset the basic rhythm, and in their determination some candidates use an over-emphatic heavy touch that is self-defeating. An ability to keep the hands in exact ensemble is needed. Examiners often hear hands starting together then parting company at difficult corners. In higher grades, part-playing will often be a feature in List A, and it's fairly rare to hear this successfully achieved. Many candidates over-emphasize the subject without adjusting the balance of the other lines. When this happens, control of dynamics and phrasing is inevitably affected.

Ornaments can be simplified or omitted in the early grades if they are causing problems with the rhythm. A steady basic beat is, of course, a higher priority than the decorations. In later grades some ornamentation is often necessary, and certainly needs to be included to achieve higher marks.

In their efforts to manage the technicalities, many candidates are less aware of the musical content of the List A pieces. It's a delight to hear the right texture, clear dynamics and musical phrasing capturing the elegant style of the repertoire, which often comes from quite an early era.

LIST B

List B gives every opportunity to show more expressive phrasing and tonal warmth. The pieces are selected mostly from the Classical or Romantic styles, and cantabile tone will be needed for the melodies. Phrasing comes right to the forefront and balance of hands needs real care, as these pieces often follow the pattern of right-hand melody and left-hand accom-paniment. Pedalling will be necessary for the more legato choices – it's expected by Grades 4 and 5, but always a bonus if managed earlier. Really clean, rhythmic legato pedalling requires good physical co-ordination, and even in higher grades we frequently hear the hands and the right foot not really coinciding.

Rubato is a vital part of musical phrasing, and is often needed in the List B pieces. Candidates are usually better at slowing up than getting faster, so it will be helpful to explain the concept of a balanced rubato dur-ing the practice period.

Dynamics tend to be more smoothly graded in the styles chosen for this list, and ability to mould the tone evenly in each hand is something to aim for at all stages. Subtlety of tone colour and control of rubato within the stylistic discipline of the pieces are high priorities. Often the pieces have descriptive titles, giving a clue to the mood and atmosphere of the music.

LIST C

This list offers something for everyone. These days there is tremendous variety – jazz pieces, contemporary items and a host of other styles – which should make it easy to find exactly the right choice for your pupils.

In the early grades the jazz items are always hugely popular. Candidates can manage quite difficult rhythms when they like the music. Strongly rhythmic, dynamic pieces, such as the all-time hit *The Swinging Sioux* from the 1999–2000 Grade 1 syllabus, seem to capture the imagination of thousands of candidates throughout the world.

With such variety on offer, it's important to go to the heart of what each piece really requires to make an effective performance. Very often this means having a feel for the underlying beat, which will be more pronounced in the jazz pieces but still vital in many contemporary items. Colourful playing, evoking the various moods and sound worlds, will be enjoyable to explore, and candidates often feel they can relax and communicate these pieces, achieving more of a sense of performance than they manage with pieces from either of the two other lists.

Swung rhythm is an issue right from Grade 1. This is not the place to give a detailed description (which really needs a demonstration to make the point), but pupils will be helped by imagining that 4/4 time becomes 12/8, so that a dotted quaver, semiquaver rhythm sounds more like crotchet, quaver. Pupils often catch on to this in certain parts of the piece, but find it difficult to be consistent, therefore causing the examiner to comment: 'Try to keep an even rhythm.' This does not mean that the swung rhythm has not been noticed, but usually indicates that there's an inconsistency in managing this throughout the performance. It is also perfectly acceptable to play the piece 'straight', especially in the lower grades, as long as the mood and relaxed feel of this style still come across. In the higher grades, the jazz pieces are quite sophisticated and really do need a sense of swing and appreciation of whichever jazz style is appropriate to the piece.

In List C the metronome mark is often that of the composer, so it pays to take notice and check carefully; as in Lists A and B, a metronome mark in square brackets indicates that it is an editorial suggestion, allowing a little more freedom of choice.

Young pupils often have a refreshingly open mind about contemporary items. Teachers may find some of the pieces slightly off-putting, but may be surprised to find that their students can get inside the music quite quickly and thoroughly enjoy playing in a different idiom.

Candidates are free to choose the order of their three pieces. It may well be wise to put the more technically demanding List A piece somewhere other than first in the exam. Many pupils these days start with their favourite piece, which helps confidence when they come to tackle the others. It is sometimes rather disappointingly obvious why a piece has been left until last!

The extensive choice for each grade should ensure that each one of your candidates is happy and comfortable with the choice and order of his or her pieces. As teachers will be well aware, the attitude of mind as a candidate comes into the exam room is inevitably reflected in the result.

Life is hectic for Anthony and me. He does his writing late at night, and I am more likely to make a 5.30am start. The commentaries on some of the grades have been written while on Associated Board business to the West Indies. Whenever or wherever our thoughts have been written down, however, it is in the hope that our experience and understanding will give you both reassurance and some new ideas. We hope that this book will be a good companion during the lifetime of this exciting new syllabus.

Clara Taylor

GRADE 1

Pupils will usually have been learning for up to eighteen months by the time Grade 1 is on the horizon. They may have taken the Prep Test during this time, in which case they will probably feel quite confident when facing this first real exam. A wide choice of pieces should help to keep motivation high, so why not have some alternatives prepared, then choose the best three as the exam approaches? The criteria for assessment for all grades are printed in *These Music Exams* – a useful source of reference for teachers.

A:1 J. W. Hässler *Tempo di Menuetto in C*

It is much easier for pupils to make a start on a new piece when the notes are nicely spread out on the page. The first four bars should be quite easily managed, once the left-hand ledger line E and F are familiar.

The biggest challenge occurs in the second of the four-bar phrases, and some patient separate practice is advisable here until the notes can be played automatically. If it is necessary to look at the keyboard at this point, it is better to focus on the right hand and to trust the left hand. After arriving safely the other side of the quavers, the minim in bar 8 needs gentle emphasis to shape the phrase. The left-hand grace note in bar 9 can be left out if it proves a problem for small hands.

To add extra polish once the notes and rhythm are safe, lean on the first note and lift the second of each of the little slurs. The suggested diminuendo at bar 8 is very effective, and you might like to end with another diminuendo in the final two bars.

Keep this dainty minuet fairly light in approach. Most pupils will need to be reminded from time to time that a minuet is a dance, but with luck they will have seen one being danced in a film or television costume drama.

A:2 Purcell *Prelude*

This prelude has real appeal for the listener. If your pupils are responsive to simple but delightful harmonic progressions, their eyes should light up when you play this piece to them.

It is a good choice for those with a less secure sense of rhythm, as it contains almost continuous quavers. Practising the quaver patterns in chords helps develop a sense of their shape. When they are articulated separately, however, it is quite likely that little gaps will occur between the seventh and eighth quavers in the opening bars until an even flow of notes from hand to hand is achieved.

Only the ornament in bar 9 interrupts the continuous movement and, yes, this decoration really should be included as written – the right-hand A sounding with the left-hand chord – in order to avoid an awkward break in the flow just before the end.

The octave shift in both hands at the end of line two is likely to feel a bit dangerous. The pupil needs to be clear which hand to look at in order for this to feel safe.

The tied notes in the last bar create a graceful arpeggio, which is best played with a little diminuendo – it is never too early to be stylish.

A:3 Witthauer *Allegretto in F*

Rhythm is the key to success here. Examiners often use the term 'well felt' to describe good rhythm. There is such a difference between playing in time and really feeling the beat, and this should be explored as soon as the notes are really under the fingers. It may be a good idea at first to count in groups of three quavers if problems occur, but a swinging two-in-a-bar is the ultimate aim. Children are particularly open to new sensations, and walking round the room with you, singing the melody and feeling the two-in-a-bar with their feet, will help them to internalize the rhythm.

Watch the timing of the left-hand octaves in bars 9 and 10 as they could easily arrive too early. It is possible to play the left hand detached at bars 7 and 15 – most pupils will anyway. Elsewhere the bass line should be legato, except for octave leaps, which can be stylishly detached.

The quiet middle section is a welcome chance for dynamic contrast. The suggested fingering works well and there are no awkward moments to disturb either hand.

Allegretto is an interesting indication of tempo, as it is rather between two speeds. In this piece it obviously means something fresh and cheerful in mood that should not cause candidates to rush ahead of the all-important beat.

A:4 Mozart *Menuett in F*

Many teachers will remember with nostalgia when they first played this famous little minuet. It has appeared in exams many times over the years yet still sounds fresh and charming.

The dance rhythm is infectious, so most pupils will pick up the pattern without difficulty. But some will tend to slow up at the triplet, in which case teachers could find suitable words to overcome this: 'Haven't you learnt your *music*?', for example, fits nicely. Repeats are not needed in exams so go straight on to the middle section, bars 9–16. To master bars 9–12 expect pupils to play from memory, and many will need to look at the keyboard for this little corner.

Phrasing is the essence of a stylish performance, so it will be important to explain the elegant use of 'feminine' endings, with the resolution on the weak beat. Each four-bar phrase ends in this way and it makes all the difference to the shape of the music. Try playing the piece without the suspensions to make the point.

The interrupted cadence at bar 20 comes as a special moment, and it is not too early to give a simple description of this harmonic surprise. The pause need not be too long – just enough to enjoy the effect.

For many pupils this will be their first piece by a famous composer, which is always an inspiring thought.

A:5 Saint-Luc *Bourrée 'The Lute Player'*

Children may not know what a lute is, but they will certainly be very familiar with guitars, so explanations should be easy. The plucked sound is suggested by the lifted third and fourth crotchets that occur in most bars. From the start, aim to make these even and delicately detached so that the all-important finger memory absorbs the physical feeling that produces the musical effect.

Playing quavers evenly is important, and the better performances will show that the first of each set of four is slightly more positive than the rest. Repetitive patterns can be charming and help the learning process, but there is also a potential for boredom. Shaping the notes is always the answer.

The bass is legato, which contrasts pleasantly with the changes of articulation in the melodic line. The suggested dynamic plan works well – just be careful that the delicate texture is not spoiled by an overdone *forte*, where it occurs. A smoothly graded crescendo during bars 10–12 will be appreciated by examiners, as tonal control at this early stage is a very promising sign for the future.

A possible trap might be to slow up in bar 16, where the left hand has a whole bar of quavers. Otherwise, the piece has no awkward corners and should have instant appeal for many pupils – some may even play the melody on a guitar.

A:6 Türk *Ballet*

This ballet is much more lively and robust than the usual popular image of classical ballet. Türk could have been thinking of an earlier type of ballet, which was more of a spectacle, at times a pantomime.

The repeated notes create a natural staccato that gives the piece sparkle. Make sure the first quaver of each bar is more important than the next three to avoid a plodding effect, which could threaten the cheerful character of the music.

Allegro non tanto (not too much) is a wise warning. It is easy to foresee performances that begin at a brisk pace for the opening section then slow right down for the right-hand semiquavers, which do actually fall comfortably under the hand; the 1-2-3-4-5-4-3 fingering is obviously the best. The weaker fingers, 4 and 5, will have to work hard as the pattern is repeated – good medicine for a developing technique.

It might be wise to suggest beginning a little less than full *forte* in bar 10, then allowing the repeated pattern to create its own crescendo. A light, crisp attack works well in this piece – too much weight would make the technical side of things hard work and take away the fun. Above all, it must sound as if the player is enjoying the piece and has a mental picture of the colourful dancers.

B:1 Beethoven *German Dance in C*

It may seem odd to start work on the left hand before the right hand, but doing so will make things much easier in the long run. So much depends on the left hand finding the characteristic oom-pa-pa chord shapes with confidence, and it is well worth patiently spending time on this; perhaps you might play the melodic line while the pupil learns to manage the bass in time.

Balance could be an issue here, as the left hand cuts across the graceful melody. However, once the left hand feels really safe, it will be able to play slightly more lightly than the right hand.

We shouldn't be conscious of the bar lines, only of the dance rhythm. It is all too easy to have a slight, often anxious, hesitation at the bar line in order to find the next note. The chords at bars 10 and 12 also need to arrive on time, and almost all players will look at the keyboard at this point. Having arrived triumphantly, we hope, on the right notes of the chords, avoid staying too long on them however great the sense of relief!

It is also important that the right-hand fingering is systematic and settled. Pupils are so prone to improvise their own, sometimes precarious, alternatives.

Although this piece contains a number of challenges, it more than repays the effort, and bears the stamp of its illustrious composer in a playful mood.

B:2 C. Gurlitt *Cradle Song*

You can always rely on Gurlitt for an appealing melody. He wrote extensively for children and had an innate understanding of what they can manage and enjoy. It is a good experience for teachers to feel that a composer is on their side.

The choice of tempo is more of an issue than it might appear – too fast and you destroy the gentle rocking suggested by the title, too slow and you lose the shape of the phrases. The editor's metronome mark of dotted crotchet = *c*.72 is ideal.

While dynamic markings give the overall level, fine adjustments are called for. The right hand needs a well-projected cantabile, at a slightly louder level than the left-hand accompaniment. Examiners hear many performances in which the melody is submerged beneath determinedly even but too heavily played left-hand quavers. The balance of hands is a key feature of the piece and is well worth early attention in the learning process.

Musically aware pupils will instinctively give the B♭ in bar 12 a little space, before the final phrase. The latter inverts the opening melody and beautifully balances the whole structure.

This piece provides an ideal opportunity for pupils to achieve subtle tone colouring, which will be needed for many other pieces.

B:3 Head *The Quiet Wood*

A professor at the Royal Academy of Music, Michael Head was a wonderfully eccentric figure, often to be seen carrying a bunch of flowers. His feeling for nature is reflected in his songs and piano pieces, and the beautiful tone he produced is at the heart of his piano writing.

In this atmospheric miniature, each hand needs a seamless legato and singing tone-quality. An efficient but insensitive performance will not get to the core of the music or gain the highest marks in an exam, so give this piece to those who will appreciate its gentleness.

Many pupils are much more aware of the right hand than the left, but here equal attention is needed in both lines, especially when the melody passes from hand to hand in bars 9–10 and 20–21.

A slow even tempo can be a challenge when exam nerves strike, and examiners sometimes hear performances played in a great rush in the heat of the moment. It will help to think of the minim two-in-a-bar beat as slow footsteps. Counting a 'bar for nothing' before starting to play can steady anxiety. If, on the other hand, you have a pupil who always prefers slow pieces to the more finger-taxing sort, this would be an ideal piece to play first in the exam.

B:4 Gedike *Cossack Song*

The notes are easy but the time signature might cause a few difficulties. In theory it is just as straightforward to play in 3/2 as in 3/4, but somehow the look of the printed notes is less clear. Children are usually quick to pick up a melody, so why not sing the tune, trying it out as a little aural repetition test, dealing with two bars at a time? That way, the pupil will have something to hold on to as they practise.

There is nothing like a 'sound picture' to help put things in place. The Russian flavour comes through the economical texture, and an explanation of the title, perhaps a picture of a Cossack, will bring this miniature to life. In addition, older pupils may find the video of *Dr Zhivago* a useful pointer, and your adult pupils will, no doubt, have already seen the film.

Pupils should aim for a wonderful legato in each hand. The unusual lengths of the phrases give the piece a unique structure. The emphasis of the first main phrase could be on the right-hand A of bar 5; the pattern repeats itself, with the phrase point again on the A, in bar 11.

The dynamic range is limited, and a mysterious atmosphere will emerge if tone quality is sensitively explored.

B:5 E. Horák *Cuckoo*

Cuckoos are rarely heard these days, but hopefully your pupils will know what they sound like. They will probably need to be reminded that the stress in the cuckoo's call falls on 'oo' not 'cuck', which means the second note falls on the first beat of the bar at each appearance.

The left hand is played entirely in the treble clef – a fact to be pointed out to less-aware students, who may spend a week at home playing the left hand in the bass, with curious results!

Pupils can easily make the mistake of playing the opening four bars in two- rather than three-time, missing out the rests on the second beat. By bar 5, however, all should settle comfortably into a regular three beats.

The contrast between a neat staccato for the cuckoo calls and a smooth legato for the more melodic passages gives the piece character. In bars 13–18 both kinds of touch are needed simultaneously – quite a new skill for many beginners and one that may take time to manage.

Repeats are not needed in exams, so it is best to practise playing straight through. Details to notice include the echoes in bars 2–4 and 20–24, the latter being harder to manage because the statement is already *piano*. Careful balancing between the hands is needed when the left hand accompanies in regular crotchets.

B:6 M. Vogel *Andante in D*

Independence of hands is a necessity for success here. Placed at the more difficult end of the spectrum for Grade 1, this piece is rewarding both for the player and listener.

The dreaded words 'separate practice' apply, and pupils, while understanding the sensible suggestion, often forget this once they are at home. The right hand of the last two bars will need lots of practice, always using the same fingering to ensure safety. It might be worth dividing the piece into sections for practice purposes, before gradually reassembling it.

The music looks faster on the page than crotchet = 92, and a fairly leisurely approach will help to avoid fingers falling over themselves. The dynamic level is gentle throughout, just rising and falling naturally with the pitch of the melody. The Alberti bass should be an accompaniment, not an intrusive feature. Pupils often laugh when teachers demonstrate a much louder left hand than right hand, but it is a great way to make the point.

Much is contained in these three attractive lines but, providing things are taken slowly and carefully in the preparation time, this piece could turn out to be a firm favourite. Teachers will know that the biggest challenges often give the most satisfying rewards.

C:1 Bartók *Wedding Song*

This is one of a set of folksongs from Slovakia, and it manages to recreate, even with a thin texture, the features characteristic of music from this region.

The fact that it is only three lines long is likely to make this piece attractive to those pupils who take a pragmatic approach! Some may also be attracted by the title, and can be encouraged to imagine a colourful country wedding.

Bartók himself tells us that the repeated notes should be played with the same finger – how sensible, as finger changing is always hazardous, even for advanced pianists. The long crescendo–diminuendo in bars 1–7 gives a lovely shape, and a similar rise and fall would be effective beginning at bar 10, peaking at bar 12, then fading away to the end. The 3/4 bar in the middle of the piece halts the duple metre for a moment; make sure the dotted crotchet has full value – it would be easy to shorten it.

The left-hand syncopation needs care – another chance for a quick clapping test, which should settle the pattern before the fingers take over.

The gentle tone and walking pace of the music should create a thoughtful atmosphere; perhaps the guests are strolling to the church rather than celebrating afterwards.

C:2 Jürgen Golle *Reigen (Round Dance)*

The catchy little tune really does sound like a children's song, and you can imagine children dancing in a circle. The 3/8 time signature should eventually sound like one in a bar, but counting three to begin with will help to make sure the left-hand chords arrive promptly, avoiding any little hesitations. Another possible trap is the 2/8 bar (bar 12), which should run immediately back into 3/8 time, without a hitch. This feels a bit strange until you get used to the sound. The left hand has an opportunity to show off an even legato and musical phrasing from bars 10–15, then moves into the bass clef for the first time at bar 16. Try to avoid a pause at this point while the chord is found.

Da capos are expected in exams, and this one ends in bar 9 with a pause, which is not needed at the first playing.

There is quite a lot of musical detail here, and although the piece has a cheerful outdoor mood, it is best in the hands of your more musically sensitive pupils, who will be able to combine a firm rhythm with subtle tone qualities.

C:3 Peter Gritton *Creepy Crawly*

Children love the jazzy List C pieces, and this one is bound to be a very popular choice. The title and the 'sinister' marking will be irresistible attractions.

The piece could be played as written or with swung rhythm, replacing the 4/4 with a feeling of 12/8. The latter seems the more stylish and relaxed approach, and it is just as straightforward to play as the printed version. Candidates sometimes give examiners mixed messages in exams by apparently 'swinging', but rather inconsistently, causing comments on the mark form such as 'It was a pity the rhythm was uneven.' The key to success lies in an absolutely solid rhythm in the bass. Watch out for any tendency to shorten the ends of bars 2, 4, 6 and 10. Feel a finger-clicking four-in-a-bar, whether swung or not.

It is worth noticing that the only *forte* as such is at the end, so make the most of the quiet moments in order to get the scariest effect.

For safety, the final left-hand C could be 'measured' by putting the thumb on the previous C an octave higher. It would be a shame to end with a blob, although, during an exam, this would be less of a disaster than the performer might think – examiners always consider the whole performance.

C:4 Absil *Carillon*

The bells ring out in both hands in this rhythmic, clear-textured little piece. It is always good news to have the same pattern throughout in the bass, as it considerably cuts down the learning time. The printed fingering surprisingly suggests 1-2-2-5, but 1-3-2-5 seems much more practical, especially for a movement that happens so many times. The right-hand bells have a minim pattern that starts at bar 7. This takes turns with the simple but colourful melody, which is first heard in the right hand starting at bar 3 and then later from bar 10.

The important considerations are tone quality and phrasing. In extrovert music such as this there may be a tendency to 'bash it out', but pupils should not overreact to the accents and aim to keep a singing sound. The phrasing will be enormously helped if it is reflected in the bass. It is so often the case that interesting musical ideas happen in the right hand while the left hand plods along at the same level, cancelling out the creative intentions.

As the dynamic range is all quite positive, it is wise not to start too loudly. A carefully judged pause on the last chord will create its own diminuendo.

C:5 John Rowcroft *The Vamp*

'Solid swing time' the composer tells us, and 'solid' is a particularly apt way to describe the appeal of such a rhythmic style. The notes are comparatively few and far between; it is the way the pulse is put across that makes the piece successful or otherwise. Here is a strong case for swinging the rhythm – feeling the quavers as if they were a lazy dotted quaver, semiquaver, dotted quaver, semiquaver, rather than the printed four quavers. The left hand walks along, emphasizing the two-in-a-bar feel, and the rests need to be exact.

The metronome suggestion of minim = 74 is an ideal tempo to conjure up the walk of this flirty lady, who would no doubt be swinging her feather boa as she strolled along, fully conscious of the effect she was creating. All this may need some explanation to your pupils. Perhaps a photograph of a 1930s Hollywood star would help – or maybe even a demonstration! Otherwise a lot of youngsters may be inclined to rush the tempo, fleet of fingers but unaware of the musical cameo the title inspires.

The quieter moment, in bars 5–7, is a vital contrast before the spirited end. To make sure of a safe last chord, practise moving the left hand into position in the crotchet rest. The ending shouldn't be too thunderous – think of a wink as the lady disappears.

C:6 Jenő Takács *Cowboy Song*

Most pupils will find the image of an American cowboy an easy way into the music, but should be reminded that the horse is moving along in a leisurely manner. So many candidates seem to be unaware of speed indications and get faster and faster as fluency builds up, sometimes completely missing the musical point in the rush. Controlling an even crotchet beat at a slowish speed is quite a skill, and a steady performance with a smooth legato in each hand and even grading of tone will be very welcome in the exam room.

The first phrase is slightly awkward for very small hands, but the printed fingering works well. Practice will be needed to get from the low chord to the higher 7th chord in bar 13 without accident.

Pedalling is a luxury not expected at this early stage, and an effective performance is quite possible without it. There is no doubt, though, that a touch here and there, especially at the chords in bar 13, would ease the way. Skip the first-time bar to end with the last two bars, which finish the piece, rather wistfully, in B minor.

GRADE 2

Lessons will have been learnt from Grade 1, and pupils will probably want to play something similar to their favourite piece from the last exam. The pacing of the preparation, not forgetting the supporting tests, will probably be easier with the experience of Grade 1 safely in the past.

A:1 Blow *Air in C*

This is an entrancing air with just a hint of a dance, and a captivating twist at the end. There may be a temptation to reject this piece because of the number of ornaments, but don't allow pupils to be put off by these. The appoggiaturas in bars 4 and 5 are particularly charming. The mordent in bar 7 is tricky and will need a light hand, but if it causes any trouble then it can be left out.

The piece could be played legato throughout, but it may sound rather airless and leaden. Instead, experiment with lightening and detaching the crotchets, matching the articulation in both hands at the beginning. Add just a little dynamic contrast, but in the last two bars, because of the thin texture, don't overdo the *forte*: use just enough to arrest the listener's attention.

The music needs to have poise, so help the pupil choose a comfortable tempo from the first note and encourage just a hint of a breath between phrases. Point out the wonderful moment in bars 10–11, when the listener expects the melody as in bars 3–4 but is led instead up to the delicious A – the highest note in the piece.

A:2 Dussek *Gavotte in F*

This jaunty and cheerful gavotte will present few problems to most pupils. The notes sit happily under the hands, which merely need to dance their way through a few F major and C major scales and broken-chord patterns. It is worth noting the ABA structure of the piece, and perhaps teaching pupils about ternary form.

Some independence of fingers is needed, so plenty of separate practice will reap huge rewards, particularly if it is musically considered and immediately begins to incorporate dynamic shading and characterful phrasing.

The editorial slurs shouldn't get in the way of the longer four-bar phrases. The music for the right hand in bar 4 can be used as an introduction to couplet phrasing. Choreograph the hand so that it drops gently on the first of the 3rds and rises on the second. This could form part of a little improvisation to consolidate the technique.

The bass notes of the left hand in bars 17–22 should be looked at in conjunction with the right-hand melody, as they shadow the phrasing. You might change the dynamic here, as suggested, as a contrast to the first half.

The melody should be kept to the fore throughout. Detaching the right-hand chord in bars 3, 11 and 27 will help to maintain the buoyancy of the music, as will observing the rests in both hands. Finish with a cheeky, staccato bottom F.

A:3 L. Mozart *Menuet in D*

This is a lovely, teasing minuet with slightly flirtatious 'written out' appoggiaturas (bars 2, 4 etc.) and shy chuckles. Despite the editorial *forte* of the opening, the whole piece needs a lightness of touch and sensitivity to balance. Perhaps keep the crotchets generally detached in both hands to contrast the couplet phrasings, triplets and semiquavers.

Do plenty of preliminary aural activities with the pupil: contrast duplets, triplets and semiquavers in clapping games, possibly with a backing CD and preferably using minuets (piano or orchestral) by other composers. Ease of movement between the three rhythmic ideas is crucial here. All upbeats should be light (although for some this may be tricky through the semiquavers), and the grace notes on the beat should be cheeky. Don't concern pupils too much with the trill in bar 7. If they can manage it, then fine, but if not it is best left out.

It is important that there is plenty of dynamic contrast and shape as well as a clearly defined balance between the hands. The left hand should be kept light and bassoon-like, avoiding stately or pompous repeated notes. The second and third beats must be progressively lighter than the first. The solo violin, you can imagine, cheerfully plays the melody, with a little 'bow' into the appoggiaturas, and a regal curtsy at the end.

A:4 Attwood *Allegretto*

If the dance-like articulation and freedom of phrasing required in some of the List A pieces does not represent your pupil's strengths, then this charming, more legato nursery rhyme-like piece may well be the answer. It does, however, make its own demands upon the performer – not least the quick leaps between phrases, which should be agile and controlled. Try some initial preparation using triads, F major perhaps, and jumping from chord to chord. Comfortable, confident movement across the keyboard, encouraged in this way, will develop a relaxed technique.

The melody is little more than an F major scale and the accompaniment figures broken chords, so a lot of the technical work is done already, one would hope. If you begin by teaching the melody aurally, listening rather than reading becomes the prime objective; this can really help a pupil appreciate the importance of melodic shape and balance between the hands.

The phrase marks should not be taken too literally, particularly if they begin to interfere with the long melodic line. The middle section relies upon its harmonic shape for interest, so encourage pupils to take note of the suggested dynamics which help this. A little ritardando at the end will finish the piece with a delightful smile.

A:5 Handel *Impertinence*

The title and G minor key of this piece are wonderfully apt. This dance is slightly insolent in character and responds well to a detached and ponderous, though not heavy, articulation. The imitative nature of the writing, perhaps implying a grumpy conversation, will demand some independence of hands as well as absolutely consistent fingering. To this end, separate practice should be a part of the preparation, but not just in the early stages; pupils should continue to develop the individual identity of each hand right through to the performance.

For an examiner, editorial commas are a dangerous addition to the page since they are so often interpreted as a pause in the musical proceedings. This may be so in much twentieth-century music, but not here: they simply imply the end of a phrase and a small breath.

Explore the phrase lengths with pupils. Write in the longer phrase marks and decide upon a dynamic shape. Most phrases end with two minims and they must be shaded carefully; far less tone is needed on the second minim. Pupils who listen the most will shape the best, so be very persistent in asking them questions about the success or otherwise of their musical intentions.

If the final trill (bar 19, where the piece reaches its slightly moody end) causes some awkwardness, then substitute a B♭ appoggiatura.

A:6 Telemann *Gayment*

Pupils with a buoyant technique and an outgoing personality will love this piece. It is a lively, energetic dance that needs charisma and enthusiasm. The brisk quavers and semiquavers require nimble fingers and a quick approach from the surface of the keys. However, this may also encourage some unwanted foreshortening of the crotchets, which can seem quite long and exposed by comparison. The rhythms may require plenty of reinforcing to help prevent this happening.

As with much Baroque music, don't take the phrasing too literally. Play the music as it sounds best on a modern instrument. In bar 3 this certainly means completely legato in the right hand until the second beat of bar 4, but with detached quavers in the left hand.

Dynamically, the first two bars should get lighter through the upbeats. The longer phrase in bars 3–4 should begin softly, with a crescendo to the first beat of bar 4, before lightening towards the end of the phrase.

Consistent fingering will help accuracy and reliability, so if errors creep in consider inappropriate fingering as the possible cause. The fingers should be used to produce a bright, sparkling tone, as the piece should dance merrily right through to the surprisingly abrupt end.

B:1 Reinecke *Allegretto*

Pupils may find the absence of a key signature reassuring in this gently humorous Allegretto, yet what it lacks in sharps and flats it makes up for in technical and musical demands.

The slightly faltering opening, reminiscent of a child's first awkward steps, needs a poise and careful articulation that contrasts with the 'never mind, dear' warmth of the next eight bars. In the latter, a clearly defined and musically shaped melody is required above a gently undulating and legato accompaniment.

The stubbornly determined and imitative middle section requires independence of the hands, yet should have an overall dynamic shape as it ascends to the top G before finally returning to a more successful and reassuring version of the opening.

The dotted rhythms will work best if the semiquaver is tucked in and almost becomes part of the next bar. The right-hand chords in bars 23–24 and 31–32 will need balancing towards the top, an excellent opportunity to develop this technique.

The dynamics need to be contrasting, but with a not too forceful *forte*, as the texture cannot really take it.

Pupils should look beyond the short, rather disruptive slurs and think in longer, legato melodic lines, particularly at the end. Here the tune should sing through and finish with a real sense of achievement.

B:2 Sandré *Un gros chagrin (A Great Sorrow)*

It is often difficult to captivate a pupil with sad slow pieces. The task is made easier, however, when pupils can relate in some way to this mood. As an aid to understanding such a piece, it may be necessary for pupils to think of an unhappy occasion, say the death of a pet rabbit. From the mournful sighs of the opening to the sobs and silences later on, this piece is full of melancholy.

It needs a colourful variety of sounds to fully convey the sorrowful atmosphere. In this piece the dynamics, articulation and expressive detail can all be taken quite literally, though with no harsh sounds on the *forte* accents.

Many performances will probably flounder on an unsteady pulse, particularly through rests and longer notes. Some appropriately 'downbeat' words, spoken in the head while holding and waiting, may help this. Bars 11 and 21–24 will need some initial help.

There are a few details that will enhance a confident performance, most of them requiring good listening skills. The first is to suppress the underlying harmonies: a decrescendo through the left-hand 3rds in the opening, for instance, to avoid intruding on the held D, and quiet second and third beats in bar 7. Secondly, where there are repeated chords (bars 8 and 16–19) the second should be lighter than the first. Thirdly, all the dynamics should be clearly distinguished.

B:3 Schumann *Gukkuk im Versteck (Cuckoo in Hiding)*

Despite its uncomplicated nature, this piece bears an intriguing title. Perhaps it refers to the fun and games as this most elusive of bird calls first from one part of the wood and then another, cunningly avoiding the gaze of the birdwatchers in the meantime.

It is not the notes that will cause problems but the rests. A lot of pupils find silence one of the most uncomfortable parts of a performance and often cut the beats short. Thinking up words and inventing a convincing story will help them not to panic, and in this instance the rests might even be fractionally (*only* fractionally) longer than marked.

The articulation and phrasing within a quiet dynamic will be important in enhancing the character of the piece, and will be mostly achieved with hands close to the keys, coupled with a subtle dynamic shading, particularly a decrescendo though bar 2 and a light upbeat in bar 3. A good awareness of the rise and fall of the hand with a relaxed wrist will help the technique.

The middle section will need some separate work, particularly in the left hand, where the bottom crotchets should be held on under light and fairly short chords. Agile fingers will be able to form a legato line by putting the fourth finger across the fifth in bar 17 – not an uncommon fingering in the more challenging repertoire a pupil may encounter later on. The pause in bar 22 can be fairly long, and the final 'Cuck-oo' should be held for its full length.

B:4 C. Gurlitt *Night Journey*

There is a sense of drama in this piece reminiscent of Schubert's *Erlkönig*, and this piece will appeal to the imagination of most of your pupils. It could be heard, for example, as a steam train rushing along under a night sky.

The interest is in the rich, foreboding left-hand melody, so the right-hand chords should be quiet and resemble a frightened heartbeat. The right hand should be kept close to the keys and moved from the wrist, using the weight of the hand to produce a reliable tone. The chords shouldn't attract attention by being too staccato, and they need to enhance the shape of the melody, staying just underneath yet following the dynamic contours. You might ask your pupil to make up some pieces using right-hand 3rds to develop the necessary control and technique.

Some rubato – such as an easing of the pulse in bar 4 – will be essential if the piece is not to sound too mechanical. The left-hand melody cries out for dynamic shape and a real legato touch, with notes clearly overlapping. Dynamics should be very contrasted and arresting in their variety.

The suggested metronome mark works well, but a little more speed is also effective, giving greater flexibility for the ritenuto at the journey's end.

B:5 Salter *Waltz*

This is an attractive yet mournful dance that will present very few technical challenges at this level. It makes musical demands nonetheless, and could be used as an opportunity to demand a polish and subtlety of control and finesse beyond anything the pupil would normally aspire to.

The gentle, lilting left hand must be unobtrusive, and the rests used to get the hand in position; a little weight on the first beat will give the piece some charm. The melody, despite the marked phrasing, could be thought of as two two-bar phrases followed by a four-bar phrase, each beautifully shaped dynamically and clearly projected above the accompaniment.

Most of the time the hands will lift together to produce a dance-like feel, but pupils should be aware of the places where this doesn't happen. The crotchets in the penultimate bar should be lightly detached.

Few pupils will have a problem playing the notes of this piece, but some candidates will instinctively allow a gentle ebb and flow. They might, for instance, take a little time in bar 8, and in bar 12 for the wonderful D♯ climax before the dancers waltz away back to their seats.

B:6 Schubert *Ecossaise in C*

The naive simplicity in the opening of this Scottish dance soon gives way to a typically Schubertian surprise and just a little drama. Our dancer is perhaps gracefully preoccupied but interrupted by a handsome young man who asks commandingly if he might join her. The answer given is up to the performer, but there is definitely a lively conversation going on in the second half of this piece.

The opening two phrases should be elegantly shaped – lightening towards the end and keeping the final quavers short but not snatched. The next four-bar phrase begins lightly but gently gets louder towards the *mezzo-forte*.

The following four bars are similarly shaped to those of the opening, but have a different personality. They are also more technically demanding, as the hands will need to jump during the quaver rest. Ideally this will be done seamlessly, without looking, but don't be afraid to encourage pupils to look at their hands while they practise. Shadow jumping – moving quickly to the next position without playing – will be an important way of acquiring confidence.

The left hand is deceptive in the opening, since the quietest beats are those with the most notes. Careful listening is required, therefore, in order to judge the sound.

Finally, decide with the pupil which is the more important in the final two bars: the chords or quavers. Then balance the hands accordingly as the young gentleman, perhaps, sweeps the dancer off her feet.

C:1 Julian Anderson *Somewhere near Cluj*

Lots of preliminary aural work needs to be done on this beautiful and evocative piece before the music is approached. Sing the tune together in phrases, perhaps putting words to it but certainly conducting or tapping it in three-in-a-bar.

The first half could almost be a duet between two violins, so both hands can be learnt separately with their own musical identity. Don't be too fussy with the phrasing: think it through in long lines and give it plenty of dynamic shape.

The second half (bar 13 onwards) begins simply, with a gently descending left hand where just a little pedal might be added if it can be reached. From bar 18 onwards the melody changes to the left hand, and the balance is a bit hard to achieve as the right-hand chords could easily get in the way. Try taking just a bar or two, asking your pupil to learn them from memory, and then experiment with the sound and technique. If the left-hand fingers are kept rounded with some weight, and the right hand moves along the surface of the keys with a relaxed hand and wrist, the melody should begin to sing through. A little rubato and breadth of tempo will conjure up the atmosphere here, and the *molto lento* in the final bar enhances the surprising, even haunting end.

C:2 Brian Chapple *March Hare*

Anyone who has seen a 'mad March hare' will absolutely understand the slightly zany 5/8 interspersed with the panting 6/8. The leaping, turning and dancing that can be seen in the spring over frosted fields is clearly portrayed here.

Pupils shouldn't be disturbed by the uncommon time signature, which can happily be subdivided 3 and 2; 'Mad as a hatter' or some such phrase works well to encourage this. Once this is comfortable, it will be important to develop a one-in-a-bar feel.

The chromatic legato lines are no trouble as long as the fingering – designed here to anticipate what comes next – is observed. Technically, bar 11 may be uneasy, the right hand needing to reposition itself fairly briskly, but if a suitably sprightly staccato is adopted the hand should spring quickly from the keys. In the final four bars, co-ordination between the hands will be easier if worked at away from the score, perhaps aurally or using the motif in bars 13–14 as the basis for some improvisation.

A positive first beat in the 5/8 and gradually getting louder through the chromatic phrases work well musically. At bar 13 a convincing *mezzo-piano* will enable a dramatic crescendo to the final, crazy leap in the air.

C:3 Vincent Huet *Herbie Funky*

It is always surprising just how little instinct many pupils show for jazz and rock styles when they have possibly heard more music in these idioms than any other. They seem to hear, but don't actually listen to, the magic ingredients that go to make these styles. Why not play them some Seventies rock and roll, discussing the drumbeat and accents? Here we have a typical straight-8s rock groove, so don't forget the count-in and the push on the second and fourth beats.

The piece is really just a rhythm section with an intro and outro (the first two and last three bars), so there are no real subtleties of nuance. It must be absolutely steady and in time. Playing along to a rock beat on a computer or electronic keyboard can transform rock and jazz performances.

A feature should be made of the dynamic contrast; the opening *forte* should not be too thick and heavy, though, and the drop to *piano* in bar 7 should be dramatic and sudden. Keep all grace notes lightly squashed into the 3rds, avoiding any percussiveness.

Most work on this piece should be done from memory, focusing on consistent and appropriate fingering, particularly in bar 7 where the predominance of black notes may be unfamiliar.

There is not much more to add – except relax and enjoy!

C:4 Terence Greaves *Three Blue Mice*

This jokey and cheeky piece will definitely be popular with the youngsters, but it will probably also be 'top of the pops' with adults taking Grade 2. Don't be deceived by its apparent nursery-rhyme simplicity, though: these mice are far from naive, and the piece presents a lot of awkward twists and turns, both musical and rhythmic.

The dotted rhythms are, of course, swung and need the 'feel' behind this, so no Mozartian triplets here. Positively encourage a slight Bill Evans 'push' on the semiquavers in bar 8, for instance.

Co-ordination between the hands in bars 11 and 12 will be all the more awkward if there is not a natural fluency in the melody. Plenty of clapping, a bit of scat-singing, perhaps, and certainly some practice away from the score getting used to the rhythms will all help.

A positive tone for the minims will set up a strong pulse, and contrasting, light, twitchy staccato crotchets – with their grace notes lightly squashed in – will help the buoyancy and character. Lots of dynamic variety, including a rich and more expansive *forte* in the last line, will enhance the bluesy character and make a 'crisis out of a drama' following the abrupt rest in bar 16. There is just time for those tails to be cut off before the less than sincere *doloroso*.

C:5 John Madden *Break In*

This wonderfully imaginative piece gives enormous scope for creative use of tone, colour and – almost more important – silence. The thief's soft trainer-shod feet in the opening bars might encourage pupils to use the 'paddy' part of the finger and, if they can reach, the pedal to capture the suspense. The staccato chords in bar 7 will need more rounded fingers. The sforzandos are in the context of a *mezzo-forte*, so nothing too accented here; save it for later on.

The rhythm in bar 6 onwards, as the thief looks around, may need internalizing, so ask pupils to clap this while counting the pulse aloud. When playing these bars the pupil should distinguish between the less anxious moments of the tenuto crotchets and the quicker staccato glint of the eye. The rests both here and following should be given at least their full value, to allow the hand time to travel to its next position.

The *fortissimo* chord should be frightening and sudden. A quick yet relaxed 'grab' of the key surface, springing out against the arm weight, will give the sound. The chord is echoed before the burglar scuttles around the corner, and we catch a final fleeting glimpse of him as his figure gets gradually smaller and more distant, blending into the night.

C:6 Stravinsky *Andantino*

This piece is beautiful in its simplicity and exactly what it proclaims: music for five fingers over five notes. The hauntingly irregular phrases, and the brief change to 3/4, will cause few problems if some suitable words are thought of, or there is plenty of experimentation with the dynamic shape of the phrases.

The right hand should always be to the fore, the left-hand chords gently throbbing underneath. Even in the second half of the piece the left-hand quavers must be kept light and get quieter through the bar; they will be heard anyway as the moving part. The control of the left hand in these bars may be a little awkward, though, as the harmony notes need to be held conscientiously, with the thumb. The commas may bring with them the temptation to put in an extra beat, but avoid this at all costs: they are only intended to mark the breath at the end of the phrase.

The general absence of dynamic markings is not a reason to play without any dynamic variety. The texture clearly doesn't support anything too loud, but do experiment and perhaps write in the markings as you and your pupil jointly decide upon them.

A slightly flexible pulse will convey the childlike charm of this piece. Don't forget to remind the pupil about the da capo, perhaps adding a gentle ritardando in the final two bars.

GRADE 3

Perhaps it is time to be a little more adventurous in the choice of pieces, now that exams are quite a familiar experience. Something of quite a different style might broaden the pupil's outlook, so do explore the alternative pieces as well as the printed selection.

A:1 Anon. *Polonaise in G minor*

Bach's youngest son, Johann Christian, almost certainly played this, along with other pieces from the same collection, as it is thought to have been written for him by members of the Bach family. It is likely that young Johann managed the tricky rhythms quite easily but maybe he, too, struggled to master the more intricate bars.

Success depends on accuracy of rhythm and steadiness of pulse, which are not necessarily the same thing. The left hand has the responsibility of keeping a regular dance-like three in a bar, while the right hand fits in neatly without disturbing the flow.

The suggested metronome mark of crotchet = *c*.92 is quite fast, but although a slightly slower speed will be preferred by some pupils, it is always important to keep the vitality of the dance, which has a strong first beat, followed by more elegant second and third crotchets.

It may be helpful to start by clapping the opening rhythm. Perhaps your pupil could clap the left-hand crotchets while you clap the right-hand rhythm, then when this is really established you could swap over. It is always more effective to have one focus at a time. Watch the rhythm in bar 4 – there is a change in the pattern that might cause a hitch. Bars 5–7 will need special care because of the syncopation. Throughout the piece there may be a temptation to slacken the semiquaver, semiquaver, quaver rhythm into a triplet, so keep it really crisp and accurate.

The bass could be either legato or lightly detached. Whichever approach is chosen, the left hand should always be a little lighter than the right-hand melody.

A:2 Zipoli *Verso in F*

Pupils usually enjoy the key of F major. There is something rather soothing and pastoral about it, and this lovely melody feels absolutely right in that key. By this stage most pupils will notice that the left hand begins in the treble clef, changing to the more normal position in bar 5. But a few might overlook this, with surprising results.

The suggested phrasing, if fluently managed, does give extra polish and shape. However, if it causes any fussy disruption to the lines, it is better to play with a smooth legato throughout. The left hand imitates the right hand, giving a conversational feeling to a piece that may be the first introduction to part playing. Examiners will be pleased to hear the dotted minims in bars 10 and 11 held for their full length. It's worth the extra care here, and for the held bass notes from bar 11 to the end.

The music is essentially easy-going and uncomplicated, so a flowing *allegretto* will have the right effect. Few pupils have a memory of metronome marks, but most will feel comfortable with the description 'a bit slower than *allegro* but faster than *andante*'.

Dynamics are in the middle range – so the *forte* should not be too assertive. Observe the quiet corner from bars 10 to 12 before the final build-up, to be played with a warm singing tone.

The piece falls into two main sections, the first concluding at bar 6 and the second taking us right through to the end. Providing the legato and note lengths are given care, this piece will give an attractive combination of physical ease and melodic enjoyment.

A:3 Hook *Allegretto*

Hook performed concertos at the age of six and composed an opera at eight, so it is not surprising that this piece calls for a well-developed technique. Give it to pupils who have good facility and enjoy running around the keyboard, showing off their agile fingers.

Allegretto is certainly a wise choice of tempo – too fast and it could all go horribly wrong under pressure. The little demisemiquaver grouping that decorates the first beat of bar 2 is the first challenge. There should be no slowing-up here; it needs to fit rhythmically with the bass.

The middle section will require lots of practice once a sensible fingering has been settled on. No doubt Hook could use any choice of fingers with equal success, but we ordinary mortals will need to make decisions and keep to them in order to secure the finger memory. It makes sense to begin the semiquaver run at bar 15 with the second finger on E, and some may prefer 2-3-1-3-1-3-2-1 in bar 17. There is nothing wrong with putting your thumb on a black note if it makes a more comfortable and even pattern.

The ornament in bar 26 looks frightening, but as long as the last two semiquavers arrive with the second left-hand quaver, all will be well.

These technique-testing pieces are sometimes given less musical consideration than the more relaxed choices, but here we have graceful classical phrasing, culminating at bars 8, 19 and the final bar. The best performances will have musical phrasing, evenly graded dynamics and a feeling that the semiquaver runs are easily achieved, even if it has taken months to get there!

A:4 J. C. F. Bach *Angloise in F*

The Bach family is certainly well represented in this list – here is another member, Johann Christoph Friederich Bach. In this instance, the composer has almost come up with a Christmas carol in the opening: there is a hint of 'In dulci jubilo' in bars 1–2, and again at bars 5–6. After this the piece goes its own way with quaver runs, mostly in the right hand, and some contrary motion in bars 11 and 19.

Children often like 6/8 rhythm and find few problems with it, but watch bar 21: it would be easy to shorten the first crotchet.

Chords at phrase-ends can be a stumbling block, especially under the pressure of an exam. It is helpful to think mostly of the top line, keeping it clear and allowing the fingers to slot into place underneath, with the minimum of fuss.

It may be a good idea to put the thumb on the right-hand F of bar 11, arriving on the B♭ of bar 12 on the fourth finger, which comfortably coincides with the left-hand fourth on E. A potentially awkward moment comes at bars 19–20. Here, the left-hand 1-4 could be replaced by 3-4, which will cause a little lift over the bar line. This type of articulation also works for the final chords of each line: for instance, the final quaver of bar 7 need not be legato and you may like to slur the first two quavers of bar 8, giving another lift before quaver three and the crotchet. This will make a few nasty corners easier to manage. Quite often a musical point can be made at the same time as overcoming a technical difficulty.

A:5 W. F. Bach *Minuet in G*

A safe performance of this minuet, with notes and rhythm in place at a reasonable tempo, will gain a pass mark, so just how much detail is necessary or desirable for a really polished account? Look at the main structure before considering the slurs and staccatos. There are two main phrases: the first peaking at the triplet in bar 7, which nicely decorates the main point, and the other starting at bar 9 and following the same pattern, with its main point at the triplet in bar 17. Keeping this is mind will give the main shape, which will be even clearer with careful dynamic contrasts.

Now to consider all those little slurs. It is easy to imagine dutiful performances in which all these small markings are carefully conveyed, but at the expense of a regular pulse and evenness in the right hand. It is often better to 'think the markings' while playing, rather than make too much of them. There are also other possibilities. For example, you may find pupils arriving on their third finger on the C of bar 10, after which a tiny separation before the E gives an alternative phrasing and a more comfortable fingering.

Minuets need to dance rather than plod along. This one is not overly lively – the tempo is *moderato* – but avoid three equally weighted crotchets in each bar, which would immediately make for a heavy-footed effect. Pupils often start off with sound musical intentions and then forget them as difficulties get in the way. Bar 9 is a good place to check that the dance feel is still in place. This is also the only quiet moment before returning to the home key for the last section.

A:6 J. W. Hässler *Allegro in C*

Both key and brevity will make this piece attractive to pupils, but a word of warning: crisp even finger articulation and good independence of hands are essential for an effective performance. The semiquaver runs need to flow easily from the fingers and be comfortably managed within quite a brisk tempo – definitely two in a bar, not four.

Given the possibility of this final outcome once the early preparation is done, there is every reason to go ahead and enjoy the cheerful melody and technical fireworks, which will impress parents and friends.

The middle section is a chance to play legato to contrast with the opening, which is detached in effect because of the repeated notes and chords. The left-hand minims in bars 9–10 are easy to overlook, but worth the effort. Just before this, at bar 7, getting the right-hand semiquavers even will also pay off, as the weaker fingers will need to be firmly and neatly in control. Returning to bars 9–10, this time for a rhythmic point, make sure the quaver, semiquaver, semiquaver patterns don't turn into triplets as the piece becomes familiar.

The last line could be a bit hazardous. Careful practice will put the right-hand runs in the finger memory, but searching for the left-hand chords could ruin the effect. Most pupils will need to look at the keyboard at this point. If you think the mordent on the left-hand C in bar 15 is too danger-ous, leave it out, but finish with a splendid flourish on the trill – the printed suggestion is easy and stylish.

B:1 Grechaninov *Lullaby*

Do you find that pupils tend to play pieces at a faster and faster speed? It's quite difficult to keep a piece at a slow tempo once the fingers feel secure, but here the *lento* indication should always be in mind.

Although the time signature is 4/4, a gentle rocking two minims to a bar will help the mood of the title. If any of your pupils is a speed merchant, try walking them slowly round the room, putting your feet down at roughly minim = 44, to give them the physical feel of the tempo.

Tone colour is all important, since the slower the tempo, the longer the sounds have to last and the better produced they have to be. A cantabile tone is needed in each hand, and paying some attention to relaxing the shoulders and releasing arm weight, which both contribute towards added sonority, would be beneficial right at the start of the learning process.

The short two-bar phrases are beautifully expressive in themselves, and add up to a touching, slightly sad overall effect. Aim for a lighter feel when both hands are in the treble clef from bars 7–10. Each set of two bars has a natural rise and fall, peaking at the first beat of the second bar.

As warmth of tone is such a priority, make sure all the tied and longer note values have their full value, especially at bars 5 and 6 where the tied crotchets might be clipped. However gentle the range of dynamics, every piece needs a tonal climax, and this could happen at bars 13–14, just before the final section.

B:2 T. Kirchner *Allegretto in C*

Lots of pupils will find their own variations on the rhythms of bars 2–4, and many teachers will be counting 'one and two, *three*' to prevent the third beat arriving early. Wrong notes and rhythms seem to become perma-nently embedded in pupils' minds (even after quite a short time of prac-tice), and it is a challenge to put the right positioning of the beat into place, erasing the mistakes. Clapping the rhythm of these bars before letting the pupil loose on their own will forestall problems in the majority of cases.

Details add a tremendous amount to the liveliness of this childhood scene. Each staccato and rest needs to be exact, and the legato sections given an obvious contrast of texture, especially bars 9–16, which form the middle section. The *sforzando* chords should not be too aggressive, and are best played with crisp energy – rather like bouncing a ball. The little grace note in bar 15 is a skittish extra that adds to the fun, providing it can be deftly managed with no delay to the beat.

The music dodges around the keyboard, so a certain amount of memory will be necessary in order to get the position changes accurate and confident.

Dynamics change frequently and need real clarity, not merging into that all-purpose *mezzo-forte* which can result from overfamiliarity. The ending is *a tempo* – a witty conclusion to a colourful, effective piece, with lots of appeal for both player and listener.

B:3 C. Mayer *Study in A minor*

It would be surprising if anyone failed to enjoy this delightful melody, which has few difficulties in terms of notes or time. So why the cautionary title 'Study'? What's the medicine?

It could be called 'a study in tonal subtlety and balance of hands', as these matters are at the heart of the piece. For a change, let's consider the left hand first. The opening is obviously an accompaniment, less projected than the melody, but at bar 3 the left hand begins to be a more equal partner, ideally with a cantabile tone and an even legato. Looking through the piece it is immediately obvious where similar, more melodic passages occur in the bass (bars 9–10 and 13–14) and require the same approach.

Quite a generous range of dynamics is explored, and the even grading and general management of tone is very much part of the educational side of this study. One passage to watch carefully is from bar 9, marked *mezzo-forte*, through to bar 15, which is *forte*. It would be dangerously easy to be too positive with the *mezzo-forte*, causing the eventual *forte* to be far too enthusiastic for the gentleness of this piece.

The phrasing falls into four-bar sections, with the main point on the first beat of the fourth bar. Pupils often think of dynamics as louds and softs marked in the music, but musical phrasing also inevitably involves subtle rising and falling, in addition to the overall level of the passage. Examiners will be delighted to hear this kind of tonal awareness and control, which is rare in the lower grades.

B:4 H. Hofmann *Schelm (Rogue)*

Neat fingerwork and accuracy at a brisk tempo are the requirements for a successful performance of this piece, which is quite demanding for the grade. However, pupils who have the right kind of facility will be prepared to put in the necessary effort as the piece is such fun. The title sends out clear signals, and examiners will be hoping that there will be a cheeky sense of humour in the playing, not just accurate notes and rhythm.

The opening quaver upbeat should be lighter than the first main beat, otherwise the music starts off with the bar lines in the wrong place. This recurs at the beginning of each main section.

The main technical requirements are a crisp staccato, with fingers close to the keys, and really evenly articulated semiquavers. The pulse ticks away in a regular two until the ritardando in bars 21–22. Notice that the last quaver of bar 22 is in time. Bars 17–18 are something of a high point, the rests underneath allowing just a little flexibility. Pupils will probably feel safer looking at the keyboard for these bars.

The dynamics are vivid and often changing. The louder levels should be bright and crisp, avoiding a heavy approach, which would spoil the mood. It pays to start the crescendo marked at bar 13 with care, so as not to overdo bars 17–18.

Careful counting at bar 31 is vital, as is a really rhythmic ending. Obviously the rogue gets away with whatever he's up to on this occasion!

B:5 Hummel *Allegretto in D*

It is quite possible to play this piece effectively without any pedal, but if your pupil has long enough legs, and is keen to try, a little pedal certainly helps the tone and colour of the music. Continuous legato pedalling is not necessary, but try little touches of direct pedal to highlight the harmonies in bars 1, 13–14, 15, 17–18 and at bars 26–28. Some pupils almost stand up in their efforts to pedal, but this is disruptive to the music and makes too much of what is in effect a luxury extra. If your pupil can use the pedal with bottom firmly on the seat, and heel on the floor, then all should be well.

A flowing tempo – another *allegretto* to be judged carefully between *allegro* and *andante* – is important. Although the piece is marked in common time, a feeling of two in a bar will avoid any chance of plodding when smooth gliding is called for.

The balance of the hands will need lots of awareness. Sometimes the left hand is accompanying, such as in the Alberti bass at the start, then at other times, such as bars 9–10, the left hand is much more of a soloist. Whatever the right hand can do, the left hand needs to do just as well: cantabile tone for the melodies, and a sense of shape to the quaver runs. Musical pupils will avoid eight absolutely equal quavers, which would be too earthbound for this elegant little piece. How they do this, however, is hard to describe.

If played with tone colour in each hand, plus some pedalling, this charming miniature will have been an excellent grounding for the future.

B:6 Rebikov *Shepherd Playing on his Pipe*

Many young pianists have also played the recorder – a helpful 'way in' to this piece, which has to conjure up the sound of the shepherd's pipe. If further sources of inspiration are called for, suggest watching *The Sound of Music* or *Heidi*. Either of these successfully evokes an alpine mood.

An expressive singing tone is required. This is quite difficult to achieve so high up the keyboard, but certainly possible with the right sound-world in mind. Bars 3 and 4 are a decorated version of the opening scene. The finger-changing on the right-hand quavers seems unnecessarily fussy, especially at this relaxed tempo. It is interesting to notice the fingering suggestion of thumb on the F♯ of bar 5.

The staccato articulation and little mordent at bar 9 come as a pleasant surprise, but make sure the left-hand chords are still given their full length to provide the harmonic background. Bar 10 returns to legato, then the staccato comes back at bar 11.

Judging the different tempi is important. The opening moderato should be quite steady. Then the tempo becomes much more playful and lively for the *allegretto*, easing back to *moderato* by means of the little improvisatory passage in bars 12–15, in which the shepherd seems to be improvising on musical ideas. The shaping of this section will tell examiners a lot about the musical make-up of the player.

Simplicity and naivety can be hard to achieve, but young players usually have a head start in these youthful qualities.

C:1 Barry Mills *Clouds*

The composer has provided performance instructions, which are as follows:

> In 'Clouds' the right pedal is kept down over long spans of music, which allows one musical event to dissolve gradually into the next, so evoking slowly changing cloud patterns. Pauses, frequent changes of time signature, and brief speeding up and slowing down in tempo add to the floating quality of the piece.

It is very reassuring to know exactly what the composer wants, and the confidence that comes from knowing that you are on the right lines will make for much more committed, convincing performances of this atmospheric, ethereal piece.

A delicacy of touch and general approach is needed. The piece is all within a small dynamic range, so it would not be an ideal choice for the robust, more boisterous pupils who rejoice in making lots of sound.

It is wise to keep to crotchet = *c*.60, and to begin counting carefully through the opening bars, which could otherwise be too vague. All the speeding up and slackening is marked clearly, and there are only three changes of pedal: at bars 7, 13 and for the final chord. The *una corda* is used throughout, so pupils need to be able to reach the pedals comfortably. The soft pedal is a mystery to many pupils, so here is a good opportunity to explain and demonstrate the difference it makes to the sound. Some pupils confuse it with the third pedal, usually a dampening, practice pedal, which is often part of the modern upright instrument.

The single notes are easily found, but the chords less so. They will need to be carefully checked, as few youngsters will arrive at the right combinations on their own.

C:2 Khachaturian *No walk today!*

The footnote reminds us that Khachaturian 'wrote in a colourful, pictorial style incorporating folk idioms from Armenia and other southern republics of the former Soviet Union'. This piece is from *Children's Album* Book 1, so a strong visual impression of playground games will set the scene.

Give this piece to pupils who have already proved able to sustain concentration and control, as there is quite a potential for losing one's place and confusing one part with another. Although a certain amount of memory must be used, it is important to stay in touch with the page. Good places to look up at the music might be bars 21, 29, 47, 51 and 74.

The quavers pass from hand to hand, so evenness and matching clarity are important. Quite often, left-hand fingers are lazier than those in the right hand, and are slower to be picked up, so avoid having two notes down at the same time in the main theme and in similar patterns.

The tempo is *allegro* but not dangerously hectic. Aim to feel an unchanging one-in-a-bar through the various contrasting ideas; have a little ritardando at bars 49–50, but a longer one in the last line.

There is quite a lot of musical detail to notice while maintaining accuracy and the even flow of the quavers. A diminuendo is harder to judge than a crescendo, especially at speed, so keep an eye on these important moments.

This piece needs a certain knack and confidence; it is not one for the cautious plodder. The left hand plays in the treble clef throughout, so there is no thick sonority but plenty of excitement and technical fireworks for the budding virtuoso.

C:3 Seiber *Tango III (Argentine)*

Here is a winner for rhythmic players who have a sense of performance. You may need to find a recording of a tango, or a photograph of a couple performing the dance, in order to introduce the character of this Argentine pastiche. Brave teachers may demonstrate, but it takes two to tango and pupils will probably be unable to partner you!

An absolutely strict left-hand rhythm – dry and exact – must continue to the end, despite the various right-hand ideas. There is a good case for asking your pupil to learn just the left hand as a starting point, while you play the melody, so that the hypnotic regularity becomes imprinted indelibly in the mind.

The first right-hand challenge is the repeated chord pattern, typical of the idiom. Fingers need to be close to the keys, while a little bounce of wrist staccato will help to avoid misfires – notes that fail to sound. It all needs to be incredibly tight and crisp, demanding a secure level of facility in this sort of style.

At bar 10 the right-hand cantabile changes the mood dramatically, but the left-hand chords still stay strict, just like a dance band. It is important to make sure that the melody comes across clearly at the top of the chords. You may need to alter the fingering in the right hand at bars 12–13 and

20–21 as the printed suggestion may be awkward for some – why not use 3-1 to 2-1 on the chords either side of the bar line?

As no pedal is needed in this piece, the finger legato needs to be firm. Independence of hands will develop through having contrasting types of touch at the same time. The final flourish is irresistible – olé!

C:4 Badings *Rondo finale*

There are not many exam pieces where hands stay relatively close together and comparatively few notes are used, but here is one. It is a gift for pupils who feel uneasy using the full extent of the keyboard, especially if they are small and have short arms.

From the musical point of view, a lot needs to be done with the repetitive patterns, otherwise boredom may set in with a vengeance. All marks of expression are vital to lift the music off the page, and the leggiero in the opening bar gives a clear lead in this respect.

The left-hand rests are important, and chords should be released on time. Some pupils will put the left-hand G-B chord in bar 2 on the first beat, and it is hard to correct the habit if not picked up early on.

From bar 16 the left hand joins in with the action and the quavers need to be evenly matched in each hand. The *espressivo* and *piano* in line 5 give a welcome change of mood and colour, but the tempo should still be *allegro vivace*, with no slackening of pace in this quieter moment.

When the theme returns for the last time, in line 6, an Alberti bass gives a different flavour. Here is another potential slowing-up point to be avoided; keeping the left hand light and legato should help.

It's asking a lot to manage a *fortissimo* three bars before the end, then a sudden diminuendo to *piano* in the final bar. This *is*, however, terrifically effective in performance.

A performance worthy of a distinction will combine technical deftness with an ability to bring a simple idea to life with a sense of fun.

C:5 Bartók *The Highway Robber*

There are vivid pictures here that will appeal strongly to dramatically inclined pupils, especially those who enjoy matching stories to music. You might imagine that the series of menacing opening 5ths in the left hand is the robber himself, and the anxious melody from bar 3 is the victim. The words '*don't* take my purse a*way*' fit rather well for extra fun. The two characters alternate, each keeping its own signature tune at different dynamics.

The marking *non legato* in bar 3 does not mean a real staccato, but more a semi-detached punchy touch, which incidentally helps the fingers to negotiate bars 4, 5 and 6. Make sure the hands are exactly together here.

At bar 9 a much more legato and plaintive version of the victim's music gives a wonderful chance for contrast of sound and mood. It may be irritating to pupils to be reminded to hold minims for their full length, and there are quite a lot of them to be noticed, but it does make a difference.

Pedal is marked each time the frightening chords appear except, surprisingly, at the very end – perhaps Bartók wanted a neat dry effect at this quiet dynamic. The dynamics form a long carefully judged diminuendo, starting loudly then falling a little in line three, down to *mezzo-piano* in line four, and lastly *piano* at the *tranquillo*, which could be a little more relaxed in tempo. It's very effective when all these levels are carefully judged.

Some candidates may give a boisterous performance, but do encourage them to fade away just as convincingly. Pupils will probably make up their own version of how the story ends; musically it seems that the robber has the last word.

C:6 Nikki Iles *While the cat's away...*

Teachers often worry about these jazz pieces. Should the rhythm be swung or played as printed? In exams either version will be accepted, and will attract the same marks, providing the treatment of the rhythm is consistent, with a solid basic beat underpinning the music. Some pieces cry out to be swung, but this one can be just as successful if played straight.

As well as being settled in approach, the rhythm needs vitality, emphasized by the frequent accents. These make their point without being too thunderous, as the texture is clear and dynamics should not be overdone.

Bars that may cause some variations in rhythm are bar 2 (watch that the tied G is given full length) and bar 3 (the rest should be exact). Once mastered, these potentially awkward rhythms should be easy when they return later in the piece.

The left-hand chords need a firm attack, as the sound must last through to the next note or chord, but the melody should still come over as the main focus for the listener. It's also worth pointing out that the accents will be different: they depend on the dynamic at that particular moment, and not all accents are *forte*. The two *mezzo-piano* passages need to be an obvious contrast to the *mezzo-forte*.

Pupils will not be too challenged by the notes; it's the rhythmic quirks that create the mood of the title and give the music such wit. There is plenty of time to find the last low D, and a bit of pedal in this bar helps to make the most of the pause. Right foot and left hand should be released together to avoid a pedal 'twang'.

GRADE 4

Many of the List B pieces will benefit from some pedal, but if legs are too short there is always an alternative piece from the extensive lists. The musical character of candidates often becomes more firmly established at this stage and they can play to their strengths, making sure the pieces are contrasted in tempo and mood.

A:1 Alcock *Gavot*

So many gavottes seem to have inspired inventiveness and imagination in composers, and this charismatic dance is no exception. The slightly questioning middle section contrasts with the cheerful opening, conversing in shapely phrases before a cheeky descending sequence heralds the return of the first two lines.

The buoyancy of this dance will depend almost wholly upon a technical freedom and an instinct for sound and articulation. If you have never done so before, this provides a good opportunity to begin the study of a piece away from the instrument. Sing through phrases with your pupil; clap them and experiment with the phrasing. It might be an idea to disregard the editorial markings and persuade pupils to write in their own. This will encourage them to listen, as well as giving them more insight into the piece and ownership of the interpretation.

It is worth noticing that the phrasing of the hands is often linked. This is particularly true of bars 3–4, where the lower notes of the right hand should match the left, perhaps even holding on under the Fs if phrasing in couplets.

There is no 'correct' Baroque sound for this piece, so let your ears be the judge. A bright right-hand tone is appropriate at the beginning, but as the melody approaches the middle register, in bars 8–10, the left hand will have to lighten to allow the right hand through. There should be a length of line throughout that can only be created by sensitive dynamic shading, achieved through subtle and flexible use of weight and fingers.

If there is one thing in the preparation that will avoid anxious moments in performance it is consistency of fingering. Often the fingering will relate to the phrasing and sound, so it should never be considered in isolation – all the more reason for nurturing the musical ideas first and then practising them within this context.

With appropriate colours, sprightly fingers, buoyant phrasing and charm, this gavotte will entrance audiences and examiners alike.

A:2 Haydn *Allegro*

This is a popular sonata movement, in which a bright and cheerful melody, reminiscent of comic opera, sings merrily over a relatively uncomplicated accompaniment. It is not a virtuoso *allegro* – too fast a tempo will destroy the humour and charm, as well as making the performance sound rather breathless.

The character of the music will be strongly enhanced by a light and clean articulation throughout. The melody should be clearly defined and contrasted with the more legato nature of the left-hand quavers, where they occur.

There are a few danger spots, and first among these is the rhythmic identity of the dotted semiquavers and triplets: there should be a clear distinction between them, and the dotted semiquavers should not sound 'swung'. There may also be a temptation to rush semiquavers that follow triplets, so a good aural sense of the difference between these is important.

The upbeats will need care if they are not to become accented. The hand will naturally want to descend on to the first note of each small phrase in the opening, so the articulation needs to be achieved from the key surface.

A subtle dynamic shape will enhance the repeated right-hand notes: a gently graded crescendo through to the semiquaver triplet will prevent them sounding rather mechanical, and will follow the natural shape of the left hand.

Where one phrase follows hard on the heels of another, such as in bars 6 and 19, be sure to finish the first elegantly and to allow a little space before the next. A jolly bassoon-like descending bass at the end finishes the piece off with character and aplomb.

A:3 Mozart *Rondo in F*

The charm and varied moods of this rondo will appeal to many pupils. Explain the structure, pointing out the changes of tonality in the episodes, and how both contrast with the cheerful main subject. A little work may be needed on the left-hand semiquavers, but beyond this there are not too many technical problems; most of the difficulties relate to listening and musical decision-making.

A light left hand, combined with a characterful and subtly shaped melody, is effective. This is particularly the case with the repeated notes of the theme, which must have a sense of musical direction yet be kept light and sprightly. There should be some convincing dynamic variety through-out, of course, but note the thin two-part texture and take care to avoid a harsh *forte* sound.

Consider different ways of phrasing the music, and don't be too influenced by editorial markings. You might experiment with a more detached approach in both hands during the opening, with a small crescendo towards the third bar. The rondo theme certainly responds well to matched articulation between the hands.

In the first episode, point out the longer four-bar phrases that aren't marked, so that the pupil has a sense of the broader architecture. Phrasing the quavers in bars 17–24 too deliberately in threes could be detrimental to the line, causing the piece to lose overall shape. In the second episode, convey the wonderful key change and extraordinary intervals, as well as the significance of balance here, keeping the left hand out of the way.

The da capo should, of course, be observed, as it is the final statement of the rondo theme and brings this captivating piece to a cheerful end.

A:4 J. S. Bach *Polonaise*

Unlike the robust example of the polonaise, this dance is poetic and refined, possessing grace and courtly charm. Its uncomplicated two-part texture will appeal to pupils, although the parts, being exposed, will require good control and musical subtlety.

A good performance will rely not just on an elegantly shaped melody but on a carefully crafted left hand, which should have its own personal-ity. It is essential to be aware of, and to bring out slightly, the 'hidden' bass line – the lower quavers. This will benefit immensely from its own phrasing, which should be unobtrusive yet result in a flowing line that enhances the melody. Consider detaching the arpeggio figures at the end of bars 4 and 8.

As with any continuous quaver line, it is vital to understand the phrase structure, not just from the musical point of view but as an aid to memory, so explore the possibilities with a pupil and don't be afraid to experiment. Treat the editorial commas as no more than an indication of where a phrase ends, and write in any decisions regarding dynamics.

It is not only independence of the hands that will achieve a musical result but independence of listening: carefully adjusting the sound in response to what one hears. To this end, it can be valuable occasionally to practise the piece with the left hand to the fore.

The ornaments are decorative and should be kept light, with the exception of the final appoggiatura where a beautiful D♯ will add just a touch of poignancy.

A:5 Handel *Gigue*

This is one of Handel's few gigues in the French style, and despite its minor key it dances merrily along, with irregular phrases and a conversational two-part texture. It has a natural two-in-a-bar feel, so a fleetness of finger and clarity of articulation are needed to convey its buoyancy. Explore a variety of phrasing with the pupil, with the intention of preventing too many strong beats in a bar, which can easily make the dance sound rather heavy-footed. Where possible, phrase the first two quavers of each first and third beat together, and articulate the others. Notice, however, how a phrase can sometimes be given extra length and direction by keeping the quavers detached.

Thoroughly secure independence of hands is required throughout, so plenty of separate practice and duet work is needed, as well as playing passages through with first the right hand and then the left hand projected to the fore. Fingering should be consistent and decisive.

The suggested articulation in bar 10 works well and will give the sequence a sense of line. Be very cautious, however, of the commas in the left hand at bars 2, 5, 9 and elsewhere. These are so often interpreted in exams as musical full stops, but in fact just highlight one possible phrase structure – a chance to breathe.

Ornaments should be light fingered and sprightly. If, however, they threaten the music's fluency, just leave them out.

A good performance will have fluency, buoyant articulation and a sense of line. An excellent performance will also have just a little rhythmic nuance, as well as dynamic shape and identity to every phrase, in order to convey the teasing humour of this characterful dance.

A:6 S. Wesley *Allegro*

This is a jolly, happy-go-lucky Allegro. It begins with a cheerful carefree tune, which is then briefly developed, almost as if questioning whether the piece really has a right to be so happy. Finally there is a return to the sunny opening.

There are few co-ordination problems here. The effectiveness of the performance will depend greatly upon characterful dynamic shading and rhythmic subtlety. The staccato quavers in bar 2 should contain only the merest hint of a strong first beat to give the four-bar phrase length, while in bar 4 the cheeky written-out appoggiaturas need just a little placing and stretching of the crotchet. The *forzando* in bar 13 must be interpreted sensitively. This is a rich, warm moment – not percussive in any way.

The middle section should be thought through in long phrases. One statement, bars 17–24, is followed by two four-bar phrases, one an echo of the other, but both with an arching dynamic shape.

In bar 33, an anticipated conventional end to the four-bar phrase is cleverly and wickedly avoided, so pupils might make a feature of this, as well as of the 'what's coming next?' nature of the final bars before the obligatory da capo.

A carefully judged balance will help convey the cheerfulness and simplicity; the left-hand accompaniment figures should be light and unobtrusive, whether staccato or legato. Any unevenness in the right-hand semiquavers needs to be avoided, so technical work may be required. The performance should have space and charm, finishing with a smile.

B:1 Godard *Premier Chagrin (First Sorrow)*

Although its ardent, though somewhat anguished, chromaticism may not immediately attract a pupil's ear, *Premier Chagrin* is one of those pieces that gradually entwines its emotional tentacles around the performer and will reap huge musical rewards.

Give the music a context. Notice the tearful rise and fall of the melodic line, the sadness inherent in the unexpectedly large intervals, the outcry as the melody reaches its highest note in bar 14, and the promise of better days to come in the final bar. It is a piece that could reflect a recent sad event and needs such a backdrop to be understood. It will particularly help the natural rubato that is so essential, yet needs a bit of encouragement in some rhythmically conscientious performers.

Technically, it is a piece that needs some careful balancing of chords and melody, particularly in bars 9–12 where the weaker fingers of the right hand need to project the line. Focus the pupil here on the sound and physical sensation of this; there is a 'feel' behind the fingers when the right sound is achieved which is memorable and will help the control. The vocal phrases should have a natural spacing at the end – a breath if you will – but elsewhere keep them legato.

The suggested pedalling is relatively straightforward, but with care – attention to balance and by foreshortening the left-hand chords – it is possible to produce a convincing performance without. Take full advantage of each rallentando to help shape the melody, and encourage a wide dynamic range.

The shorter phrases towards the end are in part questioning and reminiscent of short sobs, as the tears dry up and the smile returns.

B:2 Grieg *Watchman's Song*

This is a favourite piece of many teachers: it's descriptive and imaginative and offers scope for broadening a pupil's range of pianistic colours.

The watchman keeps up his spirit with a gentle song. All is well. Unknown to him, however, the spirits of the night follow behind in the darkness. They send shivers down his spine but disappear just as quickly, as the watchman turns around and banishes them.

The opening song is broad, comforting, and lends itself so beautifully to words that it would be foolish not to have some idea of what the watchman is singing. The melody should be given a clearly defined and eloquent vocal shape, and desperately needs some pedal (if possible) but with an astute ear to know when to change. There may be a temptation to foreshorten the minim and rests in bars 4, 8 etc., so encourage the pupil to conduct these or to count out loud.

The intermezzo is at the same tempo as the song – at bar 25 it would be easy to halve the pulse inadvertently. The arpeggio figures in the right hand are not as tricky as they seem – just a shiver up and down will do, as quietly as possible and with the lightest of articulation. Assuming the pupil's hands are large enough, it helps to cover the notes with the hand and just use the 'paddy' part of the fingers to strum across the keys.

The fanfare-like outcry from the watchman should be commanding, perhaps keeping the chords detached and aiming for a brightness of tone at the top of the chords. A dab of pedal on the semibreves will avoid any harshness of tone.

Point out to the pupil the wonderful and unexpected change of tonality and harmony in bar 48 – a last warning to the spirits before the final 'all is well'.

B:3 Hummel *Romance in G*

This is a naive, entrancing piece – essentially a cheerful song full of sunshine and carefree days. Don't be deceived by its apparent innocence, however. It requires great subtlety of balance and control, as any unevenness or unwanted accents will quickly spoil the simplicity and unsettle the listener.

Notice that Hummel has allocated a crotchet to the first note of each left-hand group in bars 1–8 and again in bars 28–31. These bass notes must be conscientiously held to enhance the harmonies.

The left hand moves around quite a lot, so playing the groups of quavers together as chords, and jumping from one to another, will be useful preparation. The melody might also be added to the chords, before finally playing the quavers as written.

The accompaniment should be delicate and unobtrusive; keeping the fingers close to the key surface will help this, with perhaps just a little more weight towards the outside of the hand. A bit more tone can be afforded to the bottom notes, as they need to last a little longer and are further away in register from the tune.

Conventionally, the right-hand semiquavers following dotted notes are played together with the left-hand triplets. If they are played as written, they will sound snatched and incongruous.

The melody must be given breadth, pliancy and plenty of dynamic shape, but pupils should be wary of the *forzando* in bar 26: rather than an accent, this signals an arrival point. Give the few ornaments that there are a little space and time; treat them as part of the melodic line, not just as decoration. Ease up just a little in tempo at the end, and aim for a warm, gentle tone to finish the piece with a loving hug.

B:4 J. F. F. Burgmüller *Ballade*

A dramatic and deservedly popular study, this ballade will appeal to pupils of all ages, and is a great showpiece at festivals if played with technical authority and bravura. It has a hint of everything: an exciting chase across fields on horseback, jumping fences on the way; a moment of slightly breathless reflection and calm; and then the final charge and capture.

Whatever the image and enthusiasm, however, all will be lost if insufficient attention is given to the technical demands of the piece, which will suit pupils with a natural facility.

Consider the semiquavers first, and probably begin with bars 87–90, where so many otherwise well-prepared and promising performances have come unstuck. They will need not only evenness but also musical shape – here a dramatic diminuendo. Fingers should be close to the keys, and practice could be done with accents on every other note, in rhythms, or in short 'sprints' of a bar's length (pausing on the first note of each bar to relax the arm). Slow, comfortable and *musical* practice is also beneficial, if musical shape and a relaxed physiology are to be achieved.

The right-hand chords, while vibrant, should be lightly played, with a slight spring in the finger from the key surface and a bit of weight to achieve a reliable tone. They would also benefit greatly from a balance towards the top, to help convey brightness and energy.

The left hand needs a personality of its own and separate practice will be beneficial at all stages of the learning process.

The tempo should be kept buoyant right through to the final, dramatic chord.

B:5 S. Heller *Waltz in F*

This is an evocative and very beautiful waltz that will captivate both teacher and pupil. It dances elegantly, provided there's a warm tone, awareness of balance and, most importantly, a reliable and astute ear to listen to the pedalling and adjust to the idiosyncrasies of the piano being used.

The old adage 'to play with the ears' is often used, but not always understood. Because every piano and room are different, it is sometimes the case that in an exam very little pedal will be needed for a piece that has required quite a lot in the lessons. Bearing this in mind should highlight just how vital it is for pupils to hold every note with the fingers for its full length, and not to rely on the pedal doing the work for them. If this is done, the pedal can lift slightly earlier if necessary, to allow the piece the necessary clarity of phrasing without breaking the line.

As the piece is a waltz, the second and third beats must be kept very light in bars 2, 4 and elsewhere. Choreograph the hands so that they fall gently into the keys on the first beat, and lift lightly thereafter.

It is the second half that will require most attention to balance. A bit more speed and support in the weaker fingers is needed to convey the line in bars 9 and 10. The accompanying quavers must not intrude, particularly in bars 11 and 12.

Beyond this, the whole piece needs a Romantic pliancy and rhythmic nuance. In the final line, all the accents should be treated musically – they are expressive, not percussive or abrupt – and the *forte* should be broad, warm and shapely.

B:6 Tchaikovsky *La nouvelle poupée (The New Doll)*

The doll of the title is traditional: loved, cradled, danced with and talked to. There is a wonderful simplicity and sensitivity to the piece, and it is an excellent choice for those who have difficulty with the pedal, as it can be played without.

It would be easy to teach much of the piece aurally at first. A pupil might sing the melody, copy phrases sung to them, experiment with dynamic shape, linger a little on different notes to hear the effect, try out words and so on. It is always astonishing how well pupils listen to the nuance of a phrase when their eyes are off the music. It is also much easier to focus a pupil on just how light the accompanying chords should be, and to encourage them to think phrases across eight bars rather than four. The more 'talkative' middle section, in particular, would benefit from this length of line, and from thinking musically through the rests.

The left-hand harmonies have a simple and easily understood pattern, and if learnt in phrases, each chord played only once, they will be quickly learnt. It will also give an opportunity to explore major/minor 3rds and other intervals.

An effective and rewarding performance will have a small amount of rhythmic ebb and flow, as well as a poetic control of the musical shape and balance. Encourage pupils to allow the melody to breathe between phrases – choice of tempo will play a part in this – and to save their softest tone until the end.

The final pause is part of the piece, even though no notes are sounding. Perhaps this is the moment when the doll is placed in the cot to fall asleep, so hold the hands still.

C:1 David Bedford *Sunset over Stac Pollaidh*

This colourful and atmospheric piece will entrance and captivate the more imaginative and sensitive pupil. The composer's notes cover almost everything you need to know about the music, but a successful performance will depend very much upon conveying the vivid picture of the landscape and peaceful mood.

The melody is very slow, so careful listening to balance and beauty of line is needed; any small blemishes will spoil the effect. Listening to the decay and ends of the notes will help the subtlety of shape. The grace notes will be awkward if the tempo is too fast – far better to take a more spacious approach, allowing just a little more time to avoid them sounding panicked and abrupt.

The left-hand distant drum beats are achieved by keeping the fingers close to the keys, with the hand and wrist very malleable. Pupils can then use some arm weight, provided they control the speed, to give a soft, velvety sound.

As the opening dynamic is *pianissimo*, it may be tempting to use *una corda*, but avoid this. Focus instead on controlling the sound until the *ppp*, where *una corda* might be used for a subtle change of timbre. Even from here the sound 'dies away', so something should be kept in reserve.

It will be important to look beyond the slurs marked in the right hand, and to think in bigger sentences. A little more weight on the first crotchet of bar 3, and less on bar 4, will give the first four bars a sense of direction.

The damper pedal should be used, if possible, to help the sound world. Avoid catching the graces by delaying the pedal change just a fraction until the main note is established. Hold the final chord until the sound dies away and the sun leaves the sky in stillness.

C:2 André Previn *Mimicry*

Confident pupils with a wicked sense of humour and enjoyment of playful rhythms will find themselves naturally drawn to this piece, full of fun and games. It falls well under the fingers, but relies on some quick, co-ordinated jumps, twists and turns to achieve the buoyant articulation, sprightly phrasing and sudden changes of dynamics. It is 'gesture' music, and will be easier to play if a pupil choreographs the physical patterns. Practise a 'sweep' of the hands up the keys in the opening bar, dropping and lifting on the couplet phrasing in bar 5, and dancing and springing out of the key with the fingers in the upbeat quavers. Bars 9 and 11 may need conditioning into the hands to keep the left-hand quavers staccato underneath the right-hand slurs.

The jumps in hand position will be so much easier if the hand moves to the next harmonies rather than just to the first note of each group. Where possible, therefore, encourage the pupil to practise in chords.

This is the sort of piece that requires constant questioning of the musical personality. A short phrase is never just that, but perhaps a 'sneer'; staccato quavers a spiteful laugh; repeated couplets a sticking out of the tongue. Characterize every phrase and avoid dulling the picture by a dry and academic reliance on the notated expressive detail.

The tone should be kept bright and alive, with chords balanced towards the top and with plenty of dynamic variety. A striking contrast between *forte* and *piano* will greatly enhance the second and last lines, and lots should be made of the crescendo and diminuendo in line 4. Make a feature of the light, cheeky end.

C:3 Alois Sarauer *Mazurka*

This fascinating and slightly quirky mazurka poses a number of rather cheeky questions, almost deliberately poking fun at the performer. It contrasts, also, somewhat comic dance steps with more contemplative phrases.

This is a perfect illustration of how important it is not to see textural detail in black and white. There are many shades of grey, not least in the opening bars, therefore it is important to take a flexible approach to the score. The opening pedal marking, for example, is quite specific but doesn't really work musically – this might be one time to put musical instinct before the detail. Interpret the staccato marking and left-hand rest literally but ignore the start of the pedal marking. Instead, the pedal can go down after the F to shift the beat eloquently on to the second crotchet, with no need for a big accent. The pedalling in bars 3 and 4 works well.

The thin texture demands a lightness of touch throughout, and, more importantly, a clearly defined top line and gentle middle textures. At no point, for instance, should the dotted rhythm be louder than the minim over the top, which, naturally, is getting softer throughout. The balance should shift noticeably to the left hand in bar 8.

With the notes learnt, the piece technically under control and the sound world understood, a pupil may well consider the piece ready. A convincing performance, however, requires so much more, in particular a rhythmic playfulness and an instinctive understanding of the 'placing' of notes. With this in mind, send pupils home with recordings of the Chopin or Szymanowski mazurkas to listen to, and then discuss them in the next lesson. Better still, help pupils discover some genuine Polish mazurkas intended for dancing, perhaps complete with original bagpipe accompaniment. It is a slightly illusive subtlety of rhythm that, once understood, will bring the performance, and dance, to life.

C:4 Kabalevsky *Toccatina*

Cellists will feel at home with the rich vocal tone needed in the melody of this deservedly popular showpiece from this wonderful Russian composer. The rich bass register is contrasted with the lighter yet vibrant right-hand chords.

The piece will suit outgoing personalities, but does require technical stamina and physical awareness to maintain the fluency, sound and tempo. The right-hand chords, for instance, are easier to play if the performer has access to a little more arm weight behind what is essentially a wrist staccato with active fingers.

Get the pupil to practise the middle section first, and to learn the chords from memory. The accidentals will take some reading, and will benefit from initial work in the lesson, focusing especially on the patterns and chromatic movement.

The left hand needs lots of confidence, personality and buoyant phrasing, so plenty of separate practice will help here, encouraging a convincing use of dynamic shape.

It will possibly take some time to achieve fluency throughout, as there may be a tendency for the right hand to seize up a little. Help the pupil to understand where time might be taken so that the right hand has a moment to relax. Explain that it is important not to force oneself through any tension that might creep in, as it can become physically ingrained. Instead, at the first signs of tension one should drop and relax the arms by the side. Once the tension has subsided, one can lift the arms and continue from where one left off.

Once fluency has been achieved, the piece will almost play itself and will be an exciting addition to a pupil's repertoire.

C:5 Prokofiev *Marche*

This is not a serious military parade here, but a humorous toy-town march full of rather clumsy soldiers, misplaced bugle calls and comic confusion. The awkwardness of the soldiers is also matched by an element of awkwardness in the writing. Most of the sounds are achieved by leaving the key surface and confidently travelling fairly large distances across the keyboard. This is particularly true of bars 12 and 14, where the left hand crosses the right, and at the end.

The whole piece should be rhythmic, with well-articulated phrasing and just a hint of rhythmic placing in the couplets. The detailed articulation is an integral part of the interpretation and should be choreographed into the hands straightaway. Hands should drop firmly but not forcefully on to the accented chords, and then lift gracefully on the following quaver.

Too boisterous a tone in the opening could destroy the character of the piece, so it should be light but with a clear balance towards the top of the right-hand chords. Make a feature of the *subito piano* in bar 9, as the band forgets the notes, and also of the trumpet call in bar 12. Grace notes are light and squashed into the 3rds – played almost together.

More virtuoso moments, such as bar 16, will need courage and conviction, and the crescendo in bars 21–26 will need careful grading so that the march doesn't become too heavy footed.

Pupils will be relieved to know that the final eight bars are merely a repeat of the beginning but an octave higher, so once they have learnt the first ten bars, point out how much of the piece they can now play. The piece should finish with aplomb and a grin.

C:6 Ronald Stevenson *Spiel*

If the amount of music to be learnt influences your pupils in their choice of piece, then they don't come much more tempting than this! There are in fact only seven bars to learn, taking repeated bars into account.

There is a sense of fun and freedom to the piece, but it will not immediately feel comfortable and easy until the technique and movements are firmly established. If the seven bars are learnt from memory, work on the control, cheerful staccato touch and left-hand jumps without the hindrance of reading the music. Listening is always more astute away from the page, and the pupil can look at the hands (not a bad thing!) and experiment with the tone and control.

To maintain the energy, the left-hand quavers will need a 'ping' to the sound, produced by a quick spring out of the key. This bounce will help the subsequent movement across the more static right hand. The piece will undoubtedly benefit from practice with accents, rhythms, a legato line and so on to help the control.

Remembering that *piano* is a range of dynamic, experiment with it, writing on the score the small crescendos and diminuendos that help give charm and shape. A little pliancy and nuance will be needed to help convey character, and will avoid making the whole piece sound too breathless. With a well-chosen tempo, a physical ease and a sense of personality the performance will sparkle.

GRADE 5

School exams often become a serious threat to practice around Grade 5, so forward planning is helpful to ease the pressure. The preparation time for this grade will need to be longer than for the previous grades, but some light pieces that are quick to absorb will help to maintain enjoyment in playing while the exam work is being systematically covered.

A:1 J. C. Bach *Minuetto*

Pupils will need to overcome any worries about ornaments to give a really stylish performance of this minuet. So often it is the look of frightening clusters of little black notes that puts youngsters off this kind of piece, while in reality the actual notes are not complex at all.

It helps to tackle the ornaments as a part of the melody, singing them as they are played. Bar 1 would sound a bit bare without a trill, and if the tempo is appropriate to a stately dance, it should be quite possible to slip in the groups of five, turning the last two into D and E, as printed.

Avoid the danger of the piece becoming an exercise in ornaments; the main elements of melody and rhythm must not take second place. The really desirable trills are those at cadences and on the second crotchet of the main theme. Others could be played as simple appoggiaturas.

You may wish to experiment with different fingering, especially as the articulation is not legato throughout. For instance, the quaver 3rds in bar 3 may be more comfortably managed with 3/1-4/2-3/1-4/2. By the time pupils reach this grade they tend to go their own way on such matters, and if alternatives produce a convincing musical effect then it is better to let them make up their own mind.

The suggested dynamics give welcome contrast and structure, and the footnotes suggest other refinements. The essentials, however, always remain: accurate notes, a strong regular pulse and graceful phrasing.

Repeats should not be played in an exam, but the da capo is an integral part of the music.

Without the ornaments this piece could well belong in a lower grade so it is well worth considering it, especially for pupils who are not confident with lots of semiquaver runs.

A:2 Kuhlau *Allegro molto*

Easy on the ear, but quite taxing for the fingers, this one will delight pupils with good finger facility and a feeling for an elegant melody.

The tempo indication *allegro molto* should be noted. It really does need to go at a lovely sparkling tempo, so those pupils with an in-built tempo 'ceiling' should be directed to another choice.

The balance between melody and accompaniment is an issue that needs attention right from the start. The hands should be able to pass the melody seamlessly from one to another in bars 16–19, 34–36 and so on, avoiding lurches as one hand stops and the other takes over.

Musical pupils will react to the impact of the changing harmonies, and will enjoy finding a more subtle colour after the double bar at bar 20. The slurring at the *con grazia* in bars 30–31 is another small but telling touch, well worth the effort. Examiners hear these refinements with great pleasure, as they are often overlooked.

Pedalling may cause some uncertainty. If played with flair at a brisk tempo, it is possible to give a successful account without the pedal, but touches of direct pedalling to warm up the harmonies would be welcome. Stay away from the pedal in semiquaver passages, which, incidentally, may tend to slow down if not watched during the practice period. At this grade it would be rare to hear a performance with skilful legato pedalling, but a pupil with good co-ordination might manage it.

Phrasing, as ever, is a vital element. By now pupils should have some idea not only of the length of phrases but also where the main points need emphasis. Finally, note the frequent dynamic indications given throughout.

A:3 John Loeillet *Minuet*

Jean Baptise Loeillet settled in London around 1705, becoming 'Mr John Loeillet', teacher of flute, oboe and harpsichord. The delicacy of these instruments can be imagined in this minuet, although it was presumably intended for solo harpsichord.

'Early music' can cause deep alarm to some teachers, who suspect they might be missing some important stylistic points, but there are no hidden dangers here. Lightness and clarity of approach, plus neat articulation, will put the piece straight into the right era. The *forte* at the start is bright and sparkling rather than heavy or declamatory. The little mordents are nearly all of the lower variety, as realized in bar 2, but later in the piece there are some upper mordents, with the middle note above rather than below. Either way, these decorations should arrive with their first notes on the beat, not preceding it.

Semiquavers occur in both hands, and it is important that they are equally clear and evenly articulated. The suggested fingering is helpful as it keeps the action mainly on the stronger fingers. It's certainly a stylish approach to detach the left-hand quavers, and this also solves some fingering decisions. The harpsichord's plucked sound is not compatible with the more modern legato cantabile, and throughout this minuet a crisp clarity of attack is important.

The choice of tempo will dictate whether the music moves along rather stodgily in three, or in a much-to-be-preferred one in a bar. A succession of notes of equal value in a bar does not mean that they should have equal weight. Pupils need to listen for, and play, lighter second and third quavers in each hand, even at a brisk tempo.

If pupils have never heard a harpsichord, the old trick of placing a sheet of newspaper over the strings of a grand piano then playing the piece will surprise and enlighten, as well as adding a lot of fun to the lesson.

A:4 G. Benda *Sonatina in G minor*

There have been several pieces by Benda in previous lists, and they always proved popular. This unusual little sonatina movement is quite introspective, although the mood is certainly not tragic and the *un poco allegretto* qualification of the *andante* marking should be taken to heart. A gentle two in a bar, with an absolutely regular beat, is the starting point. However, the frequent changes of pattern are a potential minefield, with undesirable tempo changes, caused by rushed (or sluggish) quavers, and clipped rests highly probable.

There are some challenging groups of demisemiquavers in bars 28, 29 and 31 which need to be clearly articulated within the pulse. Quite a high level of dexterity is needed to pull off this section neatly and rhythmically. Many candidates find moments such as these more manageable if they look at the keyboard and play the groups from memory.

There are many details to be considered. The suggested slurs, staccato notes and ornamentation will all add style and, incidentally, higher marks in the exam, providing the basic structure is secure.

Unless skilfully applied, pedalling is likely to blur the lines and cause more problems than it solves. It is better to rely on a beautifully legato cantabile and an even grading of tone.

The essential qualities for pupils choosing this piece are a strong sense of pulse and the patience to attend to the details. If these qualities are in place, the outlook is optimistic.

A:5 Haydn *Allegro*

Budding virtuosi should fall on this one with enthusiasm. It is a wonderful opportunity to show off an impressive finger technique, and moves along at a spanking pace. There are several semiquaver passages for the left hand, which must maintain the fast pulse without dragging. Some time spent fitting in quavers, semiquavers and then triplet semiquavers, while counting a basic crotchet pulse, will save confusion later. A common mistake is to play semiquavers slurred in twos (such as in bars 13 and 14) as if the first of each pair were dotted, which is a hard habit to break, once learnt.

The phrasing may be the last thing on pupils' minds while they are learning all these notes, but they need a sense of the shape of the piece, and of a destination. The first phrase peaks with a feminine ending in bar 5, then finishes more assertively at the cadence in bar 7. Pupils often like to have a 'phrase hunting session', marking in their own ideas in pencil, to be confirmed in the next lesson. Taking personal responsibility for these often-overlooked elements can make a great deal of difference to the performance.

Dynamic markings abound, and all should come across clearly in the playing. There are plenty of echo effects, and the contrast creates a kind of terracing, slightly reminiscent of Scarlatti's dynamics. The ever-changing levels of tone should also occur in the left hand. It is so common, especially in the technically demanding pieces, to hear the left hand going along at the same level throughout.

This could be a tremendous showpiece for confident candidates who can bring off the fireworks consistently, even under exam conditions. Just a final caution – do make sure it's fast and cheerful, not fast and furious. Exam nerves can be channelled into a positive mood with splendid effect.

A:6 Richard Jones *Giga in D minor*

This is a safe choice for almost all candidates, which proves that it is worth exploring the pieces *not* in the published graded volume. All teachers feel a sense of relief when the right piece comes to light for a pupil who has a problem with the rest of the list. Having said that, it is important to appreciate the evenness and lively tempo needed to bring this off successfully. It won't be enough to plod through accurately but much too slowly, losing the dance-like rhythm and sense of fun.

Keep the pupil's right foot firmly on the floor, as nervous, unaware pedalling could ruin some neat fingerwork. Some pupils around this level are loathe to abandon the pedal, having just learnt how to use it, but they will appreciate the clean texture, provided they get lots of encouragement and praise for progress.

The ornamentation is not complex, and the little mordents can be slipped in on the beat without making too big an issue of the decorations.

Watch the rhythm in bar 9, since the ornament may cause the left hand to start the semiquavers too soon. Pupils should be encouraged to listen throughout the piece for slight hitches in the rhythm where fingers are less secure. For some reason, the point is made far more positively if pupils notice these things for themselves.

Any pupils unfamiliar with the 12/8 time signature may need to be told that it just means four-in-a-bar. Do watch out, though, for over-enthusiastic attempts that pound out a relentless beat. This music should be light and elegant at all dynamic levels.

Once the notes are under the fingers, an enjoyable phase in the preparation is reached, during which all these apparently small considerations start to produce a really polished and musically interesting performance.

B:1 S. Heller *Etude in F*

The medicine is taken with lots of sugar in this study. Heller has a wonderful way of disguising aspects of technique with an appealing melody and texture. A beautiful cantabile right-hand tone, sensitive phrasing and careful balance of hands are all indispensable assets of good piano playing. Those pupils who think that technique means lots of notes performed at great speed can learn much by practising this gentle exercise with care and awareness.

Even at this grade rhythmic misunderstandings can happen – so watch any tendency to turn the left-hand accompanying semiquavers into triplets (starting them a fraction late then making up the tempo by hurrying). These groups are lighter than the melody, and also lighter than the quavers which come at the peak of each little surge. Beginning each group of left-hand semiquavers without a thump is one of the challenges. While on the subject of rhythmic traps, it is quite possible that some pupils, when practising alone, will alter the speed of bars 7 and 11, either by speeding up or slowing down, having temporarily lost the feel of the beat.

The little syncopations in bars 12 and 13 also need care, and should still sound lyrically expressive, not angular. 'Pedalling is left to the discretion of the player', so the footnote tells us, but the texture and mood would be hard to achieve without reliable legato pedalling; four changes in each bar will usually be necessary.

The tempo marking *andantino* should prevent slow pedestrian performances. The phrasing depends on a gentle but positive flowing towards the main point. A sense of purpose and destination is always necessary, whatever the mood of the piece. There are plenty of marks of expression and all should be clear in the playing, but the best accounts will give the impression of spontaneity, rather than of effects that have been learnt.

B:2 Lévy *Lied*

Here is a German song written by a Frenchman – how unusual! Lévy was noted for his performances of Schumann, and the Romantic influence is clear in the style of this attractive little piece.

Simplicity is hard to achieve, but the overall impression should be of a lyrical, uncomplicated melody wandering happily from hand to hand through various harmonies. A glance will tell teachers that projection of the melody over the accompaniment is the musical medicine, but it is unusual to do this within such a restrained range of dynamics. Lévy gives us clear instructions, including *sostenuto* under the opening bass melody, *più dolce*, *poco più forte* and, most telling of all, *tendrement*. You can almost hear him telling his pupils: 'Not too much. Careful. Gently. Play with affection.'

Your more robust pupils would probably feel too fenced in by all this subtlety, but introspective youngsters who have a sense of tone colour will revel in the possibilities.

Notes should be held for their full length. There is quite a lot of part playing, especially from bars 11 to 18. This passage forms the middle section of the piece and provides its emotional climax, but the high pitch of the right hand makes its own intensity, so avoid forcing the tone. Lévy has carefully put *poco più forte*, so let the firm – not stabbed – accents in the tenor line provide the foundation and do most of the dynamic work.

Young cellists will identify with this naive but extremely effective bass melody. Sometimes having the sound of another instrument in mind improves the tone quality in quite a dramatic way.

Bring the piece to a very gentle end, with each chord progressively quieter. If the last one fails to sound, there's still time to play it again, especially when the pedal is sustaining the harmony. If care is taken not to smudge the texture, legato pedalling would be a bonus, adding the final polish.

B:3 Tchaikovsky *Chant de l'alouette (Song of the Lark)*

List B contains several pieces that need delicacy of touch and good left-hand control, and this is one of them. Here we have a Russian composer imitating the style of Schumann. 'Vogel als Prophet' from *Waldscenen* may have been the inspiration, but this piece written for children is very much more straightforward in notes and in rhythm.

In an ideal performance all the triplets, and there are forty-six of them, would come off neatly, with all three notes clearly articulated at a relatively quiet tonal level. This is quite a tall order, and on this ability hangs the success or otherwise of the piece. If you have a pupil who has the dexterity and consistency required, then go ahead because the piece has few other real challenges.

With all this attention focused on the right hand, it's important to attend to the details in the bass line. This alternates between legato lines and chords, including some delicate quaver chords separated by rests, which are an essential part of the rhythm and texture.

The crescendo and diminuendo markings add structure and colour, but be careful not to go beyond the dynamic level of the section.

The left hand operates quite high up on the keyboard, helping the light, airborne mood. Unlike the serene bird of Vaughan Williams's *Lark Ascending*, this one sounds cheerfully domestic.

Pupils with small hands and short legs will fall upon this piece with relief as the hands are quite close together, there are no big stretches, and the effect is better without pedal.

The grace notes of the final passage imitate the bird's chirping call, and, again, accuracy and neatness are essential in order to bring it to an end with a flourish. It's far safer to play the last two bars looking at the keyboard, to avoid a smudge. Candidates often feel devastated by an accident at the end of a piece, but to the examiner it's the overall impression that counts.

B:4 Brahms *Waltz in D minor*

The nostalgic gentle mood of this well-known piece is far from the exhilarating ballroom waltzes of Vienna. There is no tempo indication, but a slowish languorous dance, with more than a hint of sadness, comes across from the best performances. Although leaning on the first of each pair of crotchets will help to convey the wistful espressivo, it's still important that the bar lines stay in the right place. The single bass notes have the responsibility of maintaining the rhythmic structure.

How detached should the left hand be? Semi-detached is much kinder to the music than a crisp staccato. Legato pedalling can be heard on many recordings, with the bass detached within the harmonic background. Alternatively, it is equally viable to use direct pedalling, lifting the foot with the second crotchet. The decision will have to be made on the basis of individual preference, and according to the capabilities of the pupil.

The most awkward bars are from 15–24, where the left hand will need to move swiftly and accurately across the distances without delaying the right-hand melody. The footnote points out that there is some part-playing to be appreciated during bars 17–22 and again at 25–27.

Usually we don't expect to hear repeats in an exam, but here is the exception that proves the rule. The piece is short and the material from bars 20–24 is important, providing a subtle climax with the hands quite far apart. It would be a pity to omit this, and an examiner would prefer to hear the first-time and the second-time bars. The first repeat is, however, optional. Make the decisions about the repeats early on, as there is nothing worse for the nerves than finding yourself looking at the wrong place on the page while negotiating repeated passages.

The tone quality can make or break this subtle piece, and sensitive players will also instinctively know where little touches of rubato add something memorable.

B:5 H. Hofmann *Elegie*

For once the left hand plays the starring role, acting both as soloist and accompanist while eloquently expressing the sadness of the title – although not, however, tragically or dramatically, because the mood is understated and the *andante con moto* prevents too funereal an approach.

When starting the piece, pupils may be confused by the layout on the page. 'Where exactly does the second right-hand chord go in bar 1?' Once this is explained and falls into place, the rhythm becomes predictable. Good co-ordination is always necessary with syncopations, as they can arrive too early or too late until the pupils get the knack. It may be worthwhile settling this issue in the lesson before letting the pupil loose on their own.

Being able to play at different dynamic levels simultaneously is also part of good co-ordination, and teachers will immediately spot that this skill is vital for the piece to succeed – not that the attention is always on the bass line, though. There is some duet writing in bars 9 and 10, then the right hand completes the melody at bar 11. The middle section, from bar 12 until the first beat of bar 21, contains right-hand melody with left-hand accompaniment, and there are more duet effects from bars 17–19.

Pedalling is only marked in three places, but there's no doubt that legato pedalling, changing twice per bar, would add much more polish and Romantic colour.

The main problems are likely to be difficulties with the rhythm and an over-intrusive right-hand syncopation. Sometimes such hurdles give an opportunity to work on the weaknesses and to finally overcome them. Occasionally, especially with the rhythmic side of things, it may be wise to suggest a different piece if the pupil is in danger of getting stuck and losing confidence.

In the correct hands this is a delightful choice – full of musical opportunities, while demonstrating developing skills.

B:6 Schumann *Phantasietanz (Fantastic Dance)*

For the nimble-fingered this piece is tremendous fun – certainly one with which to impress friends and family. Although it looks daunting, the technical demands are not beyond the grade, as it is beautifully written and lies under the hands (which do not have to be large ones).

'Every note. I must hear *every* note', a piano professor at the Royal Academy of Music used to say, and this is the heart of the matter. Pupils who fling themselves impetuously at the piece may enjoy it hugely as they flash around the keyboard, but a superficial fluency, with notes running into each other in a blur, may be the outcome. A firm two-in-a-bar rhythm will prevent any tendency to rush, and this, plus clarity of articulation, will go a long way towards achieving success.

There are two main musical ideas: the opening upward groups, reaching an exciting conclusion in bar 4, followed by a more lyrical second section in which the left hand needs a cantabile projection in the tenor line while the right hand echoes the melody and adds drama. Legato pedalling, changing on every quaver, is helpful in this lyrical section, but the foot should be kept firmly on the ground in the opening scale-like passages.

A lot is demanded of each hand, as the alternating groups must be equally clear. It's actually a fascinating pursuit to listen for meticulous evenness and attack on every note. Once experienced it's never forgotten – especially if the effort is rewarded by lots of praise.

Vitality and speed are not the same thing. Teachers will know which of their pupils have an inner musical energy and emotional response, and which will simply play fast. This is a piece where a 'taught' performance, with notes, time, tempo and details all in place, will convince up to a point; but the inner fire of the real musician will lift the notes off the page and take us to the fantastic realms that Schumann visited so often.

C:1 Bartók *An Evening in the Village*

Be bold with tempo changes, as the evening of the title has two very different moods. The first, a pastoral *lento*, is followed by what could well be a wild party starting at the *vivo* in bar 10. The change should come as a wonderful surprise, with the precise, tight rhythm that Hungarian dances enjoy.

Not surprisingly, two very contrasting technical approaches are required. The most beautiful legato cantabile should be used for the right-hand melody, with controlled weight on the accents, which should be sung not attacked. Then, a finger-orientated articulation is needed to create the absolute clarity of the staccato notes as well as left-hand chords of exactly the right length. (The hands need to be close to the keys for this section.) All the rests add to the rhythm, so no pedalling, please, except where marked.

A good memory for tempo is part of a musician's equipment, and examiners will be pleased to hear the same tempo for the *lento* return at *tempo primo*. Crotchet = 80 is just right – peaceful but not ponderous.

The *scherzando* passages return but at each of their appearances the dynamic level is low. Be sure, therefore, to make every note speak, as misfires causing unexpected silences would spoil the effect. At last, a broad firm tone emerges at bar 42, as if all the merrymakers join together for some singing. This section is quite robust, with legato cantabile playing in each hand, punctuated by slightly quieter chords. Bar 48 to the end presents an opportunity for some beautiful tonal grading, but make sure that there's enough substance left in the sound to make the final *ppp* a possibility.

It would be helpful to try out a few bars of each section on the exam piano before beginning the performance. In any case, this is not the piece to play first in the exam, as the candidate will need time to adapt to the instrument before bringing this off with real confidence and flair.

C:2 Mike Cornick *Bossa Nova*

We know for sure what to do with the rhythm here as the composer stipulates that the quavers are to be played evenly. If you have a recording of dance music featuring a bossa nova, play it to your pupil. This will be more useful than describing in words the insidious but regular rhythm, and the relaxed mood of this style.

The piece is not too fast. Again, we know what the composer wants (crotchet = 132), so get the metronome rather than guessing the tempo.

The core rhythm and the heart of the dance lie in the two-bar introduction. The rest and tied quaver and crotchet need to be felt as well as counted. Some pupils may take a little while before finding their way into this pattern, but persevere: once in place, the rhythm should stick.

If you're looking for potential difficulties, they will most likely be in the rhythm, as the notes are straightforward and lie comfortably under the hands. Bar 18 is one to watch, where the syncopation gives an added twist, but bars 19 and 20 should come fairly easily, providing the opening two bars of the piece have really been solved. The little grace note in bar 4 and elsewhere should add to the laid-back and easy-going mood. Again, watch out for any disruption to the rhythm at these points, but if the basic beat is in place, all should be well.

The dynamic markings are frequent and precise, and the different tonal levels will need to be carefully planned and then programmed into the physical memory.

The piece concludes as it began, hopefully at the same tempo, just easing up a little as the player relaxes into the final chord.

C:3 Harold East *Pastime Present No. 4*

You may see the composer of this one on your timetable as the examiner of your pupils. We have several composers on the panel, and they are always pleased if one of their pieces is chosen, so don't be put off!

The downward tails in the treble clef show that these notes are taken by the left hand. Both hands need to be nimble and held close to the keys so that it sounds as if only one hand is playing. The instructions 'precise' and 'detached' are useful as an indication of both technique and mood.

Levels of tone are vividly contrasted, but make sure the rhythm and tempo are confident. It's a natural human tendency to play faster at *forte* and slower at *piano*, but this would upset the momentum and vitality of the music.

The physical business of having hands very close together and sometimes crossing over is a key issue when deciding on this piece. Pupils need to be of the neat, well-co-ordinated kind, rather than long-fingered and gangly. The first can disconcertingly turn into the second after a teenage growth spurt.

The second page is quite challenging in that every semiquaver needs to be clear and even in flow. Misfires and split notes may not, however, be too disastrous, providing the rhythm stays in place, and that it is clear that the slips are made in the heat of the moment, rather than as a result of poor preparation.

Dynamics add considerable structure and colour to the *perpetuum mobile* effect, so make sure the crescendo hiding at the end of bar 32 really happens, and is followed by a beautifully judged diminuendo in bar 38 and a slight ritardando in the last two bars.

C:4 Badings *Scherzo Pastorale*

A lot of careful preparation and a cool performing nerve will be needed for this tiny piece, which will be over in a flash. Pupils will probably not flinch at the dissonances; and it seems that, once again in the Grade 5 lists, birdsong, including a minor-3rd cuckoo call, is the inspiration behind the music.

This is one of those pieces where all you need to know is on the page. The performance instructions are precise and printed exactly in the right places. Badings has given us a very clear plan of action.

Knowing what to do is one thing, but doing it is another matter, especially for pupils with fast-growing floppy fingers, who would be safer with another choice. A high level of accuracy at speed, and an unshakeable rhythm, are the basic requirements. Performances worthy of a distinction will also have vitality, a sense of communication, and the courage to bring off all the details under pressure. The way in which a candidate returns to the *a tempo* after the accelerando in the third system is particularly telling, as this is quite demanding, especially at a brisk speed.

The contrasts of touch make a huge difference to the finished performance, so aim for a neat staccato, with hands always close to the keys. The legato phrases come as a lovely surprise after all the hectic activity, so make the most of the melody that begins in the right hand at bar 17 and is supported by held notes in the bass. At the end of this passage notice the final staccato note and the three quaver rests – a number of candidates will be tempted to shorten these in the heat of the moment.

Memory will play an important part, whether or not the music is actually on the stand. Shaking fingers could wreck the performance, so choose this piece with care and knowledge of the pupil's character, musical and otherwise.

C:5 Victoria Borisova-Ollas *Silent Island*

Poise and calm in performance are rare and valuable qualities at any level, and examiners will be impressed by these attributes at Grade 5. The sparse writing skilfully creates the atmosphere of the title, and all performance details are printed exactly where needed. Nervous candidates may well find this piece makes a soothing start to their programme, giving them a chance to settle.

Do not be deceived by the apparent freedom of the opening. Here, and indeed throughout the piece, an underlying sense of a crotchet pulse is vital. Counting is essential to give continuity to the changing lengths of the bars, while a metronome will be useful to check the crotchet = *c*.104 tempo at bar 5. After this section, the various fluctuations in speed need to become a reliable part of the performance. It's so easy to forget about these instructions when the notes become familiar and the piece is almost being played from memory.

Although the writing is mostly chordal, the effect is extremely legato, so make sure the upper notes are joined by the fingers whenever possible, and that legato pedalling is used as marked. There are also some deliberate smudged effects, such as at bars 10 and 11, so careful attention to the pedalling details will be important right from the start.

The tone colour is always very subtle, with the difference between *pianissimo* and *piano* often a feature. This is asking a lot of candidates playing on an unfamiliar piano, so advise them to try out a couple of quiet chords before playing the piece in an exam.

Ask your pupils whether they think you could write down all the marks of expression from their playing. Objective listening will then probably start to happen, albeit sporadically at this stage.

This piece is a gift for players with a sense of atmosphere, and will be exam-proof once the counting is firmly in place.

C:6 Peter Jarrett *Tomorrow*

The notes are easy, but the rhythm is tricky. A really solid beat needs to be felt at a deep level – not just in the player's head – in order to give this piece continuity and rhythmic appeal.

There is certain to be need for written-out beats, vertical lines and instructions to *count* on pupils' music. Then, of course, there is the issue of the swung rhythm. Candidates will not be penalized for playing it 'straight', provided it has the right laid-back feel, but swinging the rhythm does add authenticity. It's important to be consistent in this approach, which, when awkwardly attempted, can sound like sloppy rhythm. It's the basic beat that will hold things together and make the swing convincing.

Pupils are so often reluctant to hold notes or chords for their full value. They probably don't count the length at home, and the habit then becomes hard to break. In the case of this piece there are lots of dangerous opportunities for clipped beats, so why not use some pedal, marking exactly where to put it down and where to release it. For instance, the last chords of the phrases could all be sustained with pedal. On the second page the pedalling is already marked.

The whole piece has an improvisatory, dreamy mood, like a jazz pianist idly trying out a few ideas, perhaps with half his mind on 'tomorrow'.

If you're going for a swung version, include the dotted quaver, semiquaver groups in the penultimate line, giving them a slightly lazier feel. Some pupils may have a nasty moment with the little flourish in the next bar, but the fingering is helpful and there's no hurry.

Provided the rhythm and feel of the piece are in place, this is an excellent choice for nervous players, and the mood will also help them calm down. Remember that it's always possible to play a List C piece first in the exam, before tackling the more technically orientated A and B choices.

GRADE 6

The big hurdle of Grade 5 Theory, Practical Musicianship or Grade 5 Jazz will be successfully over as work begins on Grade 6. The slightly different criteria for the higher grades, printed in *These Music Exams*, emphasize the need for the musical character, style and details to come across with conviction. Hopefully, by now the technical fluency will support these developing ideas, allowing more focus on expressive stylistic aspects.

A:1 Pescetti *Allegro*

If scintillating articulation, a natural bravura and lightness of touch are your pupil's strengths, then this spirited and cheerful Allegro is very appropriate. It sparkles energetically throughout, but needs clarity of fingerwork that can really only be achieved with the tips of the fingers and a balanced arm. No pushing into the keys is allowed here!

In fact, a really convincing performance will need a bit more than this. An ability to brighten just slightly the top right-hand notes of the alternating semiquavers in bars 7–9, 23–25 and elsewhere, and to give them a sense of line, will greatly enhance the musical direction.

Start by exploring the possible phrasing and dynamics with your pupil. It is easier and musically more sensible to begin to learn a piece in phrases rather than in bars, as it gives it a musical rather than visual structure. The dynamic and shape will also influence the mechanism your pupil will use to play a passage.

This piece begins imitatively (this same pattern occurs twice later on) but soon settles into right-hand semiquavers over a left-hand accompaniment, and there are few co-ordination problems. The left-hand phrasing could, where appropriate, be matched to that of the top notes in the right-hand passages. In bar 48, for instance, try phrasing together the right-hand D♯ and the top B with the left-hand B and G, and playing staccato thereafter. The more scalic and arpeggiaic sequences can be a little more legato and shapely. Do listen out for unwanted accents where the right hand jumps (such as in bars 40 and 42); the tone must be controlled, despite the quick movement.

Evenness of articulation will otherwise be the only technical concern. Suggest that your pupil practises by slightly accenting one note in each group, changing the emphasis each time through, and experiments with different touches and dynamics. Such work will seem worthwhile eventually, when the piece begins to glitter merrily. This Allegro is a joy to play and will be very popular in concerts.

A:2 J. S. Bach *Invention No. 15 in B minor*

The opening of this melodic yet slightly pompous dance-like invention bears an uncanny resemblance to the C minor fugue in book 1 of the '48', and provides a wonderful excuse to have a look at other Bach pieces that the pupil is not far from exploring. Try listening to a recording of the fugue and discussing not only the similarity of the notes but also the phrasing, tempo and character of the performance, as a prelude to learning this invention.

This piece is not entirely cheerful, but there is a sense of the cup being half-full rather than half-empty, and the bassoon-like left hand in the opening contrasts smugly with the rather arrogant subject.

As with all Bach's inventions, the musical rewards for the conscientious and detailed work that must be done to achieve a fluent and characterful performance are huge. Begin, though, by taking a little time to discuss the structure, phrase lengths and particular features of the piece, so that the pupil learns the notes within a framework. This will make it easier to practise in sections that make musical sense. Consistent, logical fingering will be crucial at all times. This may take a little sorting out, but it will be worth the time and effort.

The amount of playing with separate hands that is needed cannot be emphasized enough. Each hand should have complete independence of technique, phrasing, fingering and, most important, of musical personality. Encourage this before, during and after working at hands together, as the ear can so easily switch-off and the brain get obsessed with notes rather than character.

Pupils should sense and understand that each phrase has its musical identity. But be prepared to explore the possibilities with pupils and encourage them to take an interest in making musical decisions (although the editor's advice on the articulation works very well). All semiquaver runs need a clearly defined dynamic shape, but the tone must not get too heavy and ponderous: only a small amount of arm weight is necessary, and the physical movements should be choreographed to enhance the phrasing.

Ornaments work well as indicated, but should be kept light and buoyant so that they bring out the charismatic personality of this very satisfying invention.

A:3 Mozart *Andante amoroso*

It is difficult to think of this very beautiful movement as anything other than a tender and loving operatic aria (perhaps a duet), and a pupil can be in no doubt as to its intimacy and charm.

Choose a tempo – possibly a touch faster than the one suggested – that allows flexibility around those 'special' moments, but there should be no sense of rushing or breathlessness. Balance will have to be judged by listening and responding. Work with pupils to ensure that they have a particular sound in mind for every phrase, and encourage them to experiment. A musical template will inspire them to achieve the technical control and finesse needed, as well as to adjust to an unfamiliar instrument.

The first fifteen bars make up what could be an orchestral introduction. The right-hand 3rds should be balanced carefully, perhaps thinking of clarinets, as the editorial comment suggests, on top of a rich string-like left-hand harmonic support.

The melody, starting at bar 16, trips along lightly, but with a vocal quality. Every phrase and grace note should be given personality and dynamic subtlety. Be particularly aware of beginnings and ends of phrases; pupils need to hear, for instance, bars 17 and 19 as the light, naive ends of a two-bar phrase, and should avoid playing an accent on the Ds and upbeats in bars 21 and 23.

Despite the *forte* markings, balance, texture and register must always be taken into account when deciding upon the sound. Grade the dynamics carefully, and never allow a pupil to spoil the simplicity of line with too robust a tone.

The movement from duplets to triplets may prove unsettling, but less comfortable to some will probably be the sudden change from the triplets to quavers in bar 53, where quite a few pupils may rush.

Encourage the pupil to breathe (musically and perhaps literally) where appropriate. Bars 49 and 51 need time after the first semiquaver, for instance, and the poignant interruption of bars 39 and 41 would be lost if the A♭s were not prepared by easing the pulse just a little through the preceding semiquavers.

This movement is not hard technically, and provides a very useful alternative to the other, more dextrous List A pieces. To do justice to such a sublime musical gem, however, the performer will need good control and musical sensitivity.

A:4 Bečvařovský *Theme and Three Variations*

This set of variations is in the wonderfully cheeky key of B flat major. The theme could represent the somewhat scandalous flirting of a young couple, which encourages the village gossips in the first variation; is the cause of embarrassed sniggering by local children in the second; and elicits an understanding yet reproachful response from the parents in the third. Whatever musical picture you decide with the pupil, it is always valuable to characterize each variation in this way.

The tempo should be carefully considered, keeping the second variation in mind, as anything too fast is likely to result in the demisemiquavers being scrambled. Even, controlled and articulate fingerwork will be the bedrock of a bright and colourful performance. Throughout the theme the 3rds should be carefully balanced towards the top and the staccato quavers both light and short. Dynamics should be within a range suitable for the thin texture and limited register, so careful listening is essential to avoid too forceful a *forte*.

The first variation needs to be fleet of finger and effortless. The upbeat demisemiquavers should be light, with virtually no arm weight, and should contrast with the much more legato semiquavers. Grace notes and the turn are decorative and unobtrusive over subtle, controlled left-hand chords. The *forte* should be taken with a pinch of salt; let the ear be the judge to avoid a muddy texture.

The second variation has a simple opening, but is interrupted by the giggling right-hand demisemiquavers, which should bubble merrily down. The third variation is very different. The left-hand accompaniment would benefit from a true legato, with the bass notes perhaps slightly held down to provide a richer harmonic cushion beneath the melody. Certainly, the top notes of each triplet should be lighter than the first, or they are likely to intrude and distract from the melody. Try to judge whether the right-hand semiquavers sound better played as written or played with the last note of the left-hand triplet. The latter is probably preferable but may not be possible.

Sensitively shaped phrase endings and balance will enhance the charm of the piece, which should finish with a final flourish and a confident perfect cadence.

A:5 Clementi *Allegro con spirito*

If D major scales and a natural right-hand facility are the strengths of any of your pupils, then this piece is undoubtedly the choice for them. In fact, this popular and cheerful Allegro relies almost entirely upon the right-hand melody for its musical interest, contrasting legato melodic phrases with slightly teasing musical figures and bubbling semiquavers.

The subtle charm of the piece, however, will be quickly lost if due consideration is not given to the left-hand accompaniment. The opening left-hand quavers should provide a harmonic carpet, with the first of each group held for longer than its marked value and the other three played gradually lighter, so that the ear hears a balanced triad at the end of each minim beat. The lower notes are even more significant where they provide a hidden counter-melody, such as in bars 16–18.

The flirtatious opening, with its coquettish grace notes and short phrases, should contrast with the more legato second subject, where a change of colour will convey the more sensuous secret. The right-hand melody could be comic opera and the semiquaver runs coloratura, so it needs plenty of shape, space to breathe and a twinkle in the eye.

In the sequential section from bar 39 the dynamics should be graded carefully, particularly through the right-hand 3rds, and the ear focused upon the melodic line to achieve a good balance between the hands in the semiquaver figures. The repeated notes in the left hand may well bring about physical tension; even a small amount will make control of the tone difficult and the sound rather spiteful. In such cases try changing fingers, with a gentle, relaxed bounce, perhaps using 4-3-2-1. After the restraint needed here, the octaves will come as some relief and will encourage the pupil to enjoy the *subito piano* and crescendo up to the dramatic pause.

This piece requires a lot of musical decision-making and characterization. The marks of expression and articulation can form the basis of this, as long as they are interpreted and not taken too literally. With finesse and technical ease, this music is ultimately rewarding and uplifting.

A:6 Telemann *Allegro*

It is sometimes a mystery how a composer can take a couple of scales and arpeggios and craft them into a simple, attractive and entrancing piece. Here is one captivating example, though, as it boasts little more than a few

D major and A major scales and arpeggios, eloquently manipulated into a charming allegro. Ask your pupil to spot them, if only so that he or she realizes just how familiar the writing is and how well it lies under the fingers.

The tempo should not be too fast. The suggested metronome mark works very well, since it gives space for elegant phrasing and yet is not so slow as to give an unwanted feel of six-in-a-bar.

Help your pupil to resist the temptation to learn the notes first and *then* explore what is possible musically. It would be a pity, for example, to learn the semiquavers in bars 5–8 with too much rotation so that accents were produced on the As. Instead, they could be played with a musically shaped bass line produced by weighting, holding and phrasing the bass notes, yet keeping the thumb light, with virtually no rotation. It is also no harder, and indeed far more interesting, to learn the notes of the right hand with plenty of dynamic shape and subtlety, developing musical ideas while consolidating the physical patterns.

Encourage your pupil to experiment with, and decide upon, the phrasing, and to practise short phrases from memory. This will enable him or her to really appreciate the wide variety of colour, shape and articulation that is possible. Try ignoring the written phrasing; at the beginning, for example, phrase only the first two quavers of each group together.

The two-part texture cries out for a lightness of tone and a dance-like quality. Dynamic variety is essential, as is a little rhythmic nuance to help the phrasing. The transition from duplets to triplets may need attention; work away from the score will prove rewarding and help this to feel comfortable.

The turn and trill in bars 54–55 should be melodic and unhurried, adding to the character of this joyful and exciting piece, as it dances its way to the final gesture – another D major scale!

B:1 Albéniz *Tango*

This is a typically arrogant yet seductive tango, and Albéniz has succumbed to Argentine influences. Everyone will have their own idea of how the music should sound, and the subtle rhythmic nuance needed may prove elusive to some. A successful performance will require much more than a study of the text; there is so much 'unspoken' that only some familiarity with the dance will achieve the right effect. Try showing film of a tango, or playing a CD of one, and talking about the characteristics of the dance. Pupils will need help in understanding where to take time, and where to place notes.

Be aware that too much pedal will spoil the character of the music, and is likely to blur the grace notes. In bar 3, for instance, a pupil might pedal through the triplet, but keep the second beat dry and the quavers detached, delaying slightly the D major chord in bar 4 – it's a bit like going over a hump-back bridge and leaving the stomach behind. This is contrasted with the warmer and more 'smoochy' sense of line in bars 10–14.

The middle section (bars 27–43) is perhaps the hardest, and it could easily lose musical direction and purpose. Balance is the key here, conveying the conversation between the right hand and left hand in the earlier bars and within the right hand in bars 35–36, while keeping the harmonic notes light. The use of *una corda* presents its own problems. Given the slightly duller tone *una corda* produces, more rather than less weight is needed behind the fingers to bring the melody to the fore. Let the pedal change the timbre, not the dynamic. The use of the damper pedal should be judged by the sound from the piano. Different instruments and venues will need a little less or more – judging this is a skill that pupils should be beginning to acquire at this stage.

The tempo marking is spot on, as it keeps the piece moving forwards but allows scope to negotiate corners. Any hint of rhythmic rigidity in the performance will really spoil the sensuousness. The final polish will probably only come from imagining a dancing pair, so be prepared to do some dancing. Who said piano lessons weren't fun?!

B:2 Skryabin *Nuances*

Don't be fooled into believing that this (on the face of it) adult piece will only attract the more mature student; its reflective nature, warmth of personality and sensuousness may prove more appealing than you realize. There is, of course, the other distinct advantage that it is very short and not too difficult to play. It is not full of memorable melodies, but conveys colour and feeling, with evocative changes of harmony and rhythmic ebb and flow.

While the notes may not prove too arduous, especially if they are memorized as they are learnt, quite what to *do* with the notes will require a lot of consideration. The *fondu, velouté* marking provides an excellent starting point. Sing out the top line just enough to allow the longer notes to move to the quavers without losing a sense of line. The left-hand quavers need their own identity: plenty of dynamic shape and a little poignancy on the tenuto notes, but keep them generally light – as the moving part, they will always be heard.

Make pupils aware of the phrase length and natural ends to the sections, in particular bars 8, 12, and its afterthought in bar 13, and the mirroring of bars 5–6 at 9–10. Lots of time and breadth are required, but where possible the fingers must create the legato line, with the changes of pedal catching the relevant harmonies. The pedalling is not too difficult in that changes can generally occur each beat, although at times this may prove a little fussy. Explore the possibility of holding for the first two beats of a bar to give more harmonic warmth.

One common mistake in this style of music is to allow changing notes under a melody to attract the listener's ear and spoil the melodic line. In the first few bars ensure that the 3rds and 5ths in the right hand are very soft underneath the tied notes, and in the final bars that the notes between the octaves are also unobtrusive.

This is a piece for a good listener, a performer who can conjure up an atmosphere and mood as well as a colourful sound. In the right hands it will entrance and seduce the audience.

B:3 Schumann *Curiose Geschichte (Strange Story)*

'Curious and curiouser' indeed. This strange story (or dream perhaps), with more than a hint of a dance, presents a wonderful opportunity to explore all of *Kinderscenen*, if only on a recording, to see where this story fits in.

There are essentially two elements of this piece that need interpretation. First, there is the slightly ungainly dance of the opening, reminiscent of a mazurka but almost comic in its awkwardness. Then there is the much more melodic and resigned middle section, which is perhaps the grandparents shaking their heads as they realize that they can't quite keep up with these new dances. Whatever a pupil decides, a story and image are needed before the notes are learnt – only then can the right sound, rhythmic subtlety, balance and tempo be considered.

The balance should always be towards the top; only in the middle section is projection of inner lines or harmonies required. 'Voicing' of the chords to the top could perhaps be practised away from the score at first, to aid listening.

The opening rhythm should clearly show the rest, so pupils must bring up the pedal with the hand on the first quaver, and perhaps delay the subsequent semiquaver. The same applies to the rest in bar 2, and a feature should be made of the accented third beat in bar 3, although no ugly sounds are permitted! Point out the longer, unmarked phrases to pupils – such as that formed by the first four bars – to give a sense of direction.

The longer quaver lines also need plenty of shape and direction. They should be played legato, with all the harmony notes held with the fingers to allow the pedal to be changed as necessary without causing any hiccups or barren textures.

Consider the dynamic markings and aim to keep a sense of proportion. *Mezzo-forte* is just that, and with the slightly limited register anything much more will inhibit a warm tone. Take the ritardando at the end at face value, as the piece finishes with a wry smile.

B:4 Debussy *Page d'album (Albumleaf)*

A fond memory, recalled with warmth, sentiment and just a hint of nostalgia – this is Debussy at his most poetic. The piece needs a natural creativity and expression, which can easily be destroyed by a lack of understanding of the amount of pianistic colour and nuance needed, or by the use of inappropriate or awkward rubato. All expressive details, therefore, should be both 'felt' and understood.

If you include free improvisation in your lessons, and encourage a sense of rhythmic freedom and experimentation with sound in a performance, then most of your pupils will have an instinct for this wonderful music.

The opening poses its own questions and needs to begin as if it is the middle of a piece – no anxious accent on the first note, but a romantic sweep towards the fourth bar, with just a little placement of the first beat. Providing the left hand is suitably soft, and the melody well projected, the pedalling is very simple, with just a change on every first beat. Bars 7–18 should begin subtly, then move forwards, with perhaps just a small intake of breath before the dance resumes.

The opening theme is beautifully contrasted with bar 19 onwards, and the pedalling might be changed here to enhance the left-hand phrasing. A decision is needed at bar 23 as to whether to catch the left-hand crotchets with the pedal and hold them through the bar, or to change the pedal on the minim. The former is preferable, but be sure that the right-hand minims clear in the rests, and that the alto melody sings through.

The drop in dynamic level to *ppp* at the end means that the earlier *piano* and *mezzo-forte* have to be relatively rich in order for there to be a contrast.

The memory fades during the closing bars, but there is a wonderful surprise at the end: the magical F major chord, when D major is so strongly anticipated. This should be presented to the listener with the caress of someone holding out the most delicate of objects. Place the chord and aim for the most ravishing, gentle tone underneath the dying sound of the long A.

B:5 Musorgsky *Une larme (A Teardrop)*

The title of this beautiful piece will give you sufficient insight into its character: it is a melancholy song without words. Although relatively straightforward technically, the piece needs the instincts and nurturing of a naturally musical performer. Its character relies on a simplicity of line and a subdued and gentle accompaniment.

If you think the co-ordination of the sweeping left hand and vocal line may cause problems, you might choose to let your pupil cut his or her teeth on one of Mendelssohn's *Songs without Words*. The opening three bars should be expansive, and clearly balanced towards the top (easier for pupils with large hands). The left-hand arpeggio in bar 3 should die away as it ascends, so that the listener is left with a wonderful D major sonority.

The 'song' itself will need a vocal, cantabile tone and some weight behind the fingers, as well as a sense of line and musical shape. It would be inappropriate for pupils to highlight the shorter phrases as marked; they should think in terms of two-bar phrases or, in the case of bars 8–11, a four-bar phrase.

The editorial *una corda* in the middle section can be very effective, as long as the melody still sings through the pedal. The left hand needs to provide a balanced harmonic bed of sound, and maybe the hand should be weighted towards the fifth finger, keeping the top D very light. A good test is to stop playing at the end of a bar, with the pedal still held down, and listen to the chord. If the D is prominent, then it is an indication that it is likely to interfere with the melodic line.

It is essential to use the pedal throughout. This is straightforward providing all the bass notes are held with the finger long enough for the pedal to change and catch the sound, otherwise the bottom will fall out of the harmonies.

Rather than take the pedal off in bar 35, it might be better to hold it through to the end. As with all pedalling, however, the ear should be the judge.

B:6 Schubert *Scherzo (and Trio) in B flat*

This cheeky and light-hearted piece laughs and dances its way to a warmer and less energetic trio, which perhaps provides a chance for a drink (soft, of course) and some pleasant conversation before joining the dance floor again.

It is a joy to play and listen to, but will need a confidence, lightness of touch and agility around the keyboard to convey the character with sufficient ease. The left hand should be unobtrusive and technically fluent, perhaps conveying pizzicato strings by slightly weighting the bass notes. The right-hand, meanwhile, plays jokingly with the phrasing, and may even stretch the time slightly on the accented crotchets. The accents here, and in the trio, should be interpreted as a slight 'leaning' into the note to give it musical significance – anything more will ruin the charm and elegance, and be almost a kick in the shins!

Short staccato from the surface of the key, a quick finger movement and a light 'squashing' of the grace notes will help the music to laugh; just dabs of pedal on the occasional first beat or longer chord are needed to warm up the tone. Rests should be used effectively, articulating quick short phrases with confidence (as in bars 15 and 49). Don't make a feature of the slur over the triplet figures, which musically work far better when joined to the first beat of each bar and kept light.

The trio should be a complete contrast, although the texture should not be too rich and thick here – the melody must be kept to the fore. The turns should form part of the melodic line, with no unwanted accent. All the legato should be achieved with the fingers, leaving the pedal to allow the sound to blossom where needed, not where the technique lets the pupil down. The dotted quavers are just that – the temptation to turn them into triplets should be avoided.

Finally, don't neglect to remind the pupil of the da capo. On the repeat, pupils might experiment with just a little change to the musical expression and nuance – a difference in dynamic or colour, say, or a slightly longer pause.

C:1 Chick Corea *Reverie*

This is the real thing, or about as close as you can get to notated jazz. Even better, it is in a jazz style that most classically trained teachers will feel comfortable with – a piece for almost everyone. Beautiful, haunting, sad and reflective, *Reverie* has an intensity and musical depth that will stay with you long after you have finished teaching or learning it.

The rhythms are at first daunting, so do some preliminary aural work with your pupil. Lots of clapping, rhythm work, singing, playing phrases by ear, experimenting with sound and rubato (while keeping a firm pulse), counting out loud and so on are needed. The rhythmic identity is unquestionable, yet it must have an improvisatory eloquence: the listener should feel that the music is being created and composed at that moment in time.

Subtle and effective pedalling is absolutely critical to a convincing performance. Change the pedal immediately after the grace notes, triplet semiquavers or quick rhythmic motifs at ends of phrases, to give clarity and finesse. Do hold the pedal through the 'heartbeat' 5ths in the left hand, though, and where the harmonies need supporting.

The melody should be clearly projected throughout, and dynamics observed, but it will be easy to break the spell and develop intrusive upbeats. Lots of musical shape is needed at all times. Dynamically, pupils should be particularly aware of the *ppp* end, so that they do not get too soft too quickly.

The harmonies are sometimes surprising and often magical. Show pupils how to savour these moments without becoming too sentimental, certainly taking a little time but perhaps changing the tonal colour.

Despite the quasi-rubato marking, there must be a sense of pulse. You might develop a feel for this with the pupil by conducting the score away from the piano, or conducting the pupil at the piano. Any angularity will soon be noticed. Rhythmic flexibility against a pulse is rubato, but rhythmic flexibility with no awareness of pulse is simply playing out of time.

A truly magical piece, enjoy it!

C:2 Martinů *Columbine Dances*

Charm, wit, humour, entertainment – this piece has it all. It is quite well known, but not often performed by young pianists. There may be good reason for this, namely the rather devious left hand. It requires excellent keyboard geography, and a courage and confidence of the most outgoing or studious of your pupils. It is musically so worth the effort, though, that it would be worth encouraging any pupil whom you consider suitable to play it.

The opening – thankfully repeated exactly, after the middle section – is a comic waltz: puppets skidding around stage with a loose-limbed swagger, revolving round and round until dizzy. The left hand will lose all its imagery if played too strictly in time; in the opening, for example, making a slight hiatus on the second beat of the bar will greatly enhance the picture, as will moving the right-hand chromatic lines forward in bars 5–9 and elsewhere. This does, though, rely upon the left hand being secure so that it can follow the right-hand melodic shape where necessary. Lots of separate left-hand practice, not looking at the hand, will help this. Thinking of all the movements as gestures will help confidence: a sweep across the arpeggiated first bar, and a rise and fall from the first-beat crotchet to the minim chord elsewhere, though avoiding a harsh accent. Make sure the hand stays in the key long enough on the crotchet to allow the pedal to change and support the note.

The puppeteers appear to get their wires crossed in the squabbling middle section, which should be energetic and bright, with left-hand chords short and clear, not heavy. To achieve the sound, encourage active fingers from the surface of the key. The melody and 4ths in the right hand should be legato – as some sense of order is restored to the puppets – and consider adding pedal again, if discreetly, from bar 35, despite the earlier *senza Ped.* marking. Dabs of pedal on the left-hand chords from bar 27 onwards will also help the sound and character.

With a technical freedom and confidence, as well as a vivid imagination, the piece will almost play itself, and be a popular and entertaining concert piece (whether used for the exam or not).

C:3 Julian Yu *Yellow Beanleaves*

Don't in any way be put off this evocative piece by the one-stave notation. In fact, there is very little to learn here, except how to read the ledger lines, and certainly there is little that is unconventional, except perhaps the harmonies. The composer's notes say all that is needed about the character, but from a learning perspective this is one of those pieces that will need some initial aural work. The piece will also be more quickly learnt if the notes are 'hung' on a firm awareness of the rhythm and articulation.

It could be learnt in short rhythmic phrases, by first counting the pulse while clapping the rhythms, and then exploring the articulation, dynamics and accents in each phrase on or away from the instrument. Do this until it is instinctive and natural. Once the scaffolding is in place, it is simply a matter of putting the correct notes on the appropriate beat.

Don't be afraid to encourage the use of some pedal, but do make sure it is not used to obscure poor note-learning, articulation or rhythmic clarity. It should, instead, enhance what is there.

The left hand and right hand can be learnt independently if this helps, but as the piece is so full of detail the markings should all be interpreted and internalized as the notes are learnt. A staccato, *forte*, *piano* or accented note is no harder to learn than one without musical identity, so do put these in straightaway.

Note, in particular, the independence of dynamic markings between the hands, and ensure that the rests are observed. The *sforzando* markings are slightly percussive and distinctive in their sound, so the chords should be made a feature of.

Once all is prepared, pupils need to be encouraged to 'let go' and enjoy all the syncopated rhythms, vivid contrasts of dynamics, phrasing, accents etc. They need to develop a physical 'groove' to the music.

It is an exciting and fascinating piece to play and will reward patient work.

C:4 John McLeod *Interlude 1*

Sometimes pupils begin a piece and thereby commit themselves to a lot of work only to find that the piece, in the end, isn't sufficiently musically rewarding. This will not be the case here – this haunting, slightly melancholy yet endearing piece will appeal to the emotions and satisfy the most demanding of students.

It will rely for its effectiveness on a neatness of fingerwork, clarity, balance, and just a touch of tearful rhythmic nuance. Any rushing of triplets, or an unpredictable pulse, will spoil the sense of spaciousness and sadness.

The opening right-hand figures should not be too heavy or laboured. A clarity of attack, without weight, is needed to allow the quick demisemiquavers to have their own rhythmic identity, followed by a smooth sense of line and the decrescendo of a long sigh. The left-hand melodies, which imitate the right-hand line, should be projected – a conversing between father and son perhaps – and all dynamics carefully graded and considered.

Be particularly conscious of the *ppp* at the end: pupils will need to establish a reliable tone here and then work backwards through the louder dynamics. All accompanying chords and harmonies must be kept right out of the way to give freedom to shape the melody.

Pedal, although not marked, will be needed throughout. It is implied in bars 5, 12–15 etc. by the writing. Elsewhere, the chords can be 'warmed up' with legato pedalling. Consider carefully whether to pedal through the demisemiquavers, however. The pedal could be lifted just before them (with the left-hand harmonies held carefully with the hand) and placed just after their articulation, soon after the second semiquaver beat.

Much valuable time may be spent away from the piano, conducting the piece through while singing the rhythm (if not the notes), to help a pupil feel at ease with the seamless, improvisatory style of the writing.

The final bars are an expression of what might have been, and the hands should be held still for the pause in the last bar, the ear listening to the sound dying away before the hands and pedal are gently lifted together.

C:5 Poul Ruders *Shooting Stars*

This is a glittering and interesting piece – almost minimalist in style. If, as the composer suggests, you have a pupil who has, or needs to develop, an effortless, crisp finger staccato, then this is certainly a good piece to consider. In the right hands it also has a strong visual image, not perhaps of shooting stars, but that wonderful 'twinkle' of bright stars in a cold winter's night sky.

The tempo should be carefully chosen, particularly as the opening bars can be played far faster than the following quavers. A pupil should have the latter in mind before starting.

The technique, not the notes, is the main challenge initially, together with the mental stamina to avoid a physical tightening of the arm. The staccato is achieved close to the key surface, with a small bounce at the wrist on to active finger tips. If the 'paddy' part of the finger is used, the staccato will be far too stodgy.

Before leaving pupils to their own devices for the week, make sure you work during the lesson on achieving the right sound through correct, balanced and relaxed mechanism. If any tension creeps in, then they should stop, drop the arms by their side and, once the tension has disappeared, continue from where they left off. This will hopefully avoid the brain making too many connections between a particular passage and muscular tension.

The hands should be balanced slightly towards the top, and the highest notes brightened just a little in the pedalled passages – these could be the shooting stars of the title.

The absence of dynamic markings does not, of course, mean that a small range should not be introduced, indeed encouraged, within the perceived phrases.

The short ritardando at the end can be enjoyed, and the final rest made just that little more significant as morning approaches and the last star disappears.

C:6 Aulis Sallinen *King Lear's Distant War*

Cunning salesmanship may be needed to 'sell' this to your pupils, but it can be done in the knowledge that this excellent piece has a lot of drama and strong imagery.

The opening, surprisingly reminiscent of Rachmaninoff's Second Piano Concerto, is full of foreboding and dark war clouds. The military march begins in the left hand, and is interrupted by sharp, stabbing and sword-slashing right-hand syncopated notes.

The chromatic *poco tenuto* motifs provide a sense of guilt and anguish amidst the pride-driven battles. Whether these feelings are Cordelia's or King Lear's is open to interpretation, but the discussion should encourage a colourful and convincing performance.

Despite the lack of an appropriate marking, pedal the opening chords, grading the dynamic carefully and counting conscientiously so that the crotchet chords have a rhythmic context. After this introduction, however, avoid pedal until marked, focusing instead on an exciting and vibrant tone in the left-hand chords, removing the hands fairly quickly from the keys (particularly important where hands share the same note).

The right-hand notes can, and should, be slightly longer, providing a war-like melody. Notice here that the C in bar 10 is tied right through. The pedal is added and changed, where marked, and the change of mood conveyed with a more vocal line in the right hand. This line is legato and should be musically shaped.

The final 13 bars are a gradual dying away. Each phrase should be at a different dynamic, bearing in mind the final *pianissimo* and that the melody will need musical shape and personality. Pupils may have a tendency to undercount the final few bars. Encourage the opposite, as the audience awaits the final chord, which perhaps portrays the pointlessness and poignancy of a war between father and daughter, and their final demise.

GRADE 7

The final grades should be equally rewarding to teachers, pupils and parents, whose involvement in the exams should be bearing fruit. The playing usually sounds quite accomplished even at a pass level, while merit and distinction categories will acknowledge musical and polished performances of real artistic quality. The highest marks most frequently go to candidates choosing pieces within their own technical comfort zone, so that expressive details and communication can lift the music off the page.

A:1 C. P. E. Bach *Allegro in A*

Choice of tempo matters more than usual, because of the need to find a brisk, but not frantic, two-in-a-bar. Extremists among your pupils – those that rush at everything, or those that plod along – might find difficulty in adapting their natural tendencies. Crotchet = 108 is just right, and allows the ornamentation to be fitted in comfortably. Played without decoration this piece would certainly be relatively easy for the grade, but with the mordents and trills more is demanded in terms of finger dexterity and consistent awareness of the pulse.

Notice that the mordents in bar 3 are of the lower variety, while that in bar 4 is of the upper, emphasizing the main point of the first four-bar phrase. Bars 5, 7 and 8 have potential rhythmic traps, and the pupil's inner hold on a regular four-crotchet pattern will keep things in shape while the ornaments are fitted in.

The chosen tempo will, of course, help determine the kind of touch needed. In this case there's no need to strive for an unvaried legato, although the appearance of the quaver patterns might suggest this. The marked fingering, mainly drawn from the original source, has implications for the phrasing. For example, the second finger after the octave leap in bar 3 and elsewhere clearly makes a legato approach impossible, and is one of the clues as to whether quavers should be slurred in pairs. The frequent repeated notes cause this 'lift' to happen naturally, so take the hint and discover the stylish feel such details contribute.

There are no printed dynamics, so you are free to make your own plans, following the harmonic structure of the piece. For instance, the opening twelve bars might be played at a bright *mezzo-forte* with, of course, the small variations caused by phrasing. After the conclusion of this section in the dominant, you might suggest a gentler start, dropping to *piano* from bar 13. From bar 24 onwards, the music moves into more obscure keys, automatically creating different colours. We return to the tonic at bar 44, at which point the dynamic could be more affirmative.

A sudden blackout, or loss of concentration, can bring a piece such as this to an unexpected stop. This is not necessarily a major disaster; a quick recovery is always appreciated and respected by examiners. A clear understanding of the harmonies (including writing them in on the music) will help the memory and provide signposts when temporarily lost.

A:2 Handel *Fantasia in C*

What an enticing start, and one that will make the pupil want to learn more. The robust simple melody in C major will appeal to most, and the subsequent patterns of semiquavers alternating between the hands are rather addictive once the rotary action is mastered. This sideways rocking of the wrist, which prevents tension and helps an even flow, must be balanced by precise fingertips – if not, the rotary freedom can get out of control. The action is small; in fact, less is more when operating at this lively tempo.

It is also important to notice where the rotary action in the right hand gives way to melodic semiquavers, such as at bar 10, where the more usual finger action, with a still wrist, is appropriate.

An invigorating rhythm is easy to achieve at the opening but could be lost later. It needs to be a very positive aspect of the piece throughout, and is marvellous for giving structure and providing something reassuring to hang on to.

No dynamics are marked, although only a rare or timid candidate would start *piano* with such a sturdy theme. In the higher grades it is best not to be prescriptive about dynamics, which can sound 'taught', rather than felt, or rather cosmetic when being dutifully obeyed. It is better by far to discuss the mood, harmonies and general impact of each section with your pupil, and let the variety of tone stem from the music itself. Beware, however, of the often-heard all-purpose *mezzo-forte* when musical intentions are forgotten in the heat of the moment or through overfamiliarity.

Equal facility, flexibility of technical approach and attention to detail are needed in each hand. Those strongly right-handed players, who struggle with demands made of their left hands, would be advised to choose something else.

The phrasing is particularly important, with so many repeated patterns. Pencilled in phrase marks are always more effective than saying: 'Think in four bars.' There is no predictable pattern here in the number of bars, which is part of its charm, so make some mutual decisions, mark them in the score and show them in the playing.

There are quite a few left-hand rests, which need to be rhythmically exact. Trills, where marked, are welcome, providing the momentum is not upset. Bars 37–44 will need lots of careful practice. This is the most demanding part of the piece, but as it is beautifully written, the notes lie comfortably under the hands.

This Fantasia is bound to be one of the hits of Grade 7, and rightly so. It has manageable demands and many rewards.

A:3 Haydn *Moderato*

'Sweet Lass of Richmond Hill', by Thomas Arne, might come to mind (especially for teachers in the UK), but only for the first bar; thereafter Haydn takes us off in other directions. It's quite unusual for a first movement of a sonata to be marked *moderato*, but in this case it is most appropriate: there's a wealth of triplets and other detailed patterns that are an integral part of the melody, not just decoration. Surprisingly, even at Grade 7 it's possible for pupils to misunderstand a rhythm and come up with what might sound a reasonable alternative. The first triplet, if the tiny *3* is not noticed, might be played as ordinary semiquavers, thereby distorting the rhythmic shape. (This would, however, sort itself out when the more obvious rhythmic pattern of bar 4 is reached.) At bars 12–13 the right-hand demisemiquavers must start firmly on the beat, and not be played as an upbeat to the left-hand octave. Apart from these two features, the rhythm should present no problem. The basic evenness and vitality of the pulse will be important in underpinning the elegant Classical writing.

Slurring in pairs is marked from bar 17 onwards, but this will happen automatically if the repeated notes are played with a light, crisp attack. Heaviness in any form is to be avoided, particularly when the left hand has accompanying chords (such as at bars 23–26). A delicate approach is also needed for bars 45–46, where Haydn has a sudden flight of fancy between established ideas. The right-hand octaves in bars 48–53 will benefit from rotary wrist action, making sure, of course, that there's no slackening of the momentum at these moments.

The development contains some tricky corners, especially bars 84–89. There is a danger that the pupil will slow down to fit in the trills in the first three bars, then have difficulty re-establishing the triplets at bar 87. The left-hand quavers here and in similar passages could be either legato or detached – the *moderato* tempo makes either approach viable.

It's often the case that List A pieces, which are usually the most technically demanding, suffer from a lack of character and mood, however efficient and well-practised the fingerwork may be. This movement is outgoing and cheerful, almost out-of-doors music, with birdsong suggested by the triplets. From one of Haydn's early sonatas, it doesn't hint at the drama and depth to come in later works. As such, it's a delightful, uncomplicated choice for pupils possessing clear articulation and good rhythm.

A:4 J. S. Bach *Gigue*

Bach's music is an acquired taste for many youngsters, but a few may already be fascinated by the masterful construction and part-writing of his music. Bach's pieces always take longer to learn, and although this gigue is only two pages long, work will have to begin in plenty of time for it to be fully absorbed. Certainly this piece is not something to change to in the final month!

A gigue should be irresistible in its lively dance rhythm, with the first beat in each bar giving a lovely vitality, and the 3/8 time signature always feeling as one in a bar.

Listening to recordings of great pianists will not only give an invaluable sound picture at which to aim but will also reveal different approaches to articulation. Examiners will accept any of these preferences, providing the musical effect is consistent and convincing.

Nimble fingers, good co-ordination, a light crisp attack and a well-felt pulse are essential qualities. The part-writing will need to be pointed out and marked where it is hidden among the semiquaver groups. In the opening bars there are a few helpful editorial marks that make things clearer. The two commas are not pauses but an indication to lift the previous note, thereby illuminating the part that follows the commas. In bars 4 and 5 the right-hand F♯ then B should be brought out, as they continue the subject. The pattern of notes remains more or less the same until bar 9, where the semiquavers form a background to the new quaver line in the bass. These quavers could be detached, but a legato touch is preferable, so as to show the effect of the commas. For instance, in bars 15 and 16 the first two left-hand quavers could be staccato, then the octave Ds slurred, with the lower one lifted, thus directing our ears to the subject appearing on the subsequent A and F♯. Similar details appear throughout the piece, and it's wise to search them out so that the physical memory can programme in the articulation.

Passages in which both hands have simultaneous semiquavers will need to be in immaculate ensemble. Watch out that the left hand doesn't lag slightly behind, or that these bars don't lose momentum. You may like to experiment with different fingering – the simpler the better, with as much matching in the right hand and left hand as possible. This will raise the safety level in performance. Balance of hands is another fundamental issue to be attended to early on.

Once thoroughly mastered, this short but complex dance is very satisfying to play – and the preparation is excellent musical medicine.

A:5 Beethoven *Bagatelle in C*

To those who hear this piece before seeing the music, it might come as a surprise to find that the skittish little opening figure is actually *on* the beat, and not an upbeat. It's easy to play this as if the right-hand E is the first main beat, but this distorts the rhythmic pattern. It is a tiny misunderstanding, easily put right.

The 'Scherzo' and 'Allegro' markings should be in mind right through the piece. Both the *minore* section and the trio should maintain the tempo, despite their contrasting contents.

Very little pedal, if any, need be used in the opening sixteen bars. The alternating detached work and single bars of legato (bars 2, 6, 10 and 12) make a sparkling impression, light and cheerful but never trivial – after all this is Beethoven!

The mood changes significantly with the *minore* section, and here legato pedalling would be advisable. The left-hand triplets must be an accompaniment, and guard against a thunderous bass intruding on the expressive cantabile melody. The *fortissimo,* at bar 24, falling back to *piano* in bar 25, is a chance for quite advanced tonal control.

So many pupils of all ages struggle with twos against threes. Bar 20 has just this cross-rhythm, and it really does need to be exact, with only the right-hand octave Cs coinciding with the left-hand As. It's frustrating when pupils so nearly get it right, then slip back to their own approximation. Independence of hands is part of the equation, and perhaps this is the piece that will finally sort out this hurdle forever.

There is another change of style in the trio, but this should still be at the opening tempo. The double 3rds, which are among the scale requirements for this grade, do not have to be perfectly legato here (what a relief!), but they do require even articulation, with consistent clarity of the top line. Imagine a cello section playing the bass at bar 52, with separate bows on each quaver, then match this with the right-hand 3rds.

Repeats are not required in exams, and, in any case, the length and changing patterns of this well-known scherzo are enough to challenge the player's concentration.

On the last page, the staccato wedge above the left-hand chords should not be too heavy or abrupt. For the last line, a beautifully judged diminuendo would be much appreciated.

A:6 Mozart *Allegro*

Teachers will remember the glow of pride when they first reached the stage of playing a sonata by a great composer. For some candidates this movement will be their own milestone, and hopefully this will encourage them to learn the rest of the piece in due course.

The gentle opening melody may suggest a slower tempo than *allegro*, but don't be lulled into an *andante*. The typically Mozartian semiquavers that soon appear would sound laboured at a less lively speed. One of the frequent hazards in Mozart is a tendency to change the tempo with the changing patterns in the music. Examiners will probably hear a cautious slackening around bars 16–22, where hands may have trouble keeping together, then a speeding up at the easier section, that is from bar 23 onwards. A useful tip is to ask the pupil to sing the opening melody and then compare that tempo to the speed of the passage causing trouble. We're all aware that if not tackled early on, this sort of tempo variation is hard to correct, with some problem bars never quite catching up.

The stylistic features of Mozart are well known, and a worthwhile exercise is to ask your pupil to list them, filling in any gaps yourself. Musically well-informed students will come up with some or all of the following: a clear light texture, not much pedal, nothing too aggressive in tone, a constant tempo, rubato only within the pulse, graceful phrasing (often with feminine endings), and changes of mood within the same piece. You may think of many more elements, but if those listed above are in place the performance is well on the way to a distinction.

Details such as slurs and rests should all be observed. Hopefully, left-hand rests will not be overlooked, and all chances to show a change of articulation should be taken. For instance, bars 31–34 are full of instructions, and the legato in bars 45 and 46 is a lovely change after the semiquavers. Watch out for any loss of tempo with the trills in bars 43 and 44, and if these are a stumbling block just play mordents in the right hand.

A high level of technical fluency and security has to be in place for this piece to succeed, as there is nowhere to hide in the event of uneven runs, stumbles or lack of definition in the fingerwork. Having mentioned the possible drawbacks, it has to be said that prolonged contact with Mozart's music will be a terrific experience, with many benefits both now and in the pupil's future playing.

B:1 S. Heller *Etude in A*

Both the staccato dots and the rhythmic dots in the music need to be understood and appreciated before the almost eastern European dance flavour of this piece is realized. Let us consider the bass first. The staccato first crotchet in each bar gives a rhythmic kick that continues until bar 32, although the staccato marks run out after bar 3. The pattern is resumed at bar 45, while the previous two bars are legato. The left hand will need to cover quite a large distance between the first and second crotchets, and pupils will probably need some encouragement to move quickly across the gap.

The double dots in the right-hand melody also give tremendous bite and character to the music, not dissimilar to that of some of Chopin's piano pieces. The semiquavers should be slipped in just before the third crotchet.

The footnote tells us that pedal is left to the discretion of the player, and although the piece might just work without pedal – if the tempo were brisk – few candidates are likely to take this option. It's quite possible to give the detached emphasis needed on the first crotchet within a legato pedal, and this is likely to be the preference of most candidates.

This is a dance with plenty of spirit and quite a bold range of dynamics. It would be good to hear a sensitive delicacy at one end of the tonal spectrum and a vivid *forte* at the other. Bars 57–60 will probably come off best if played looking at the keyboard. The continuous quavers of the coda, although marked *piano*, require no loss of intensity or tempo, and lead to an exciting final upward flourish. The last chords are most effective if played in time.

There's a lot to commend this choice. As a study, it focuses on articulation, and the right hand gets a thorough workout with a mixture of scales and arpeggios. Pupils are likely to enjoy themselves hugely once the notes and tempo are mastered, and it would be an ideal piece for school concerts or festivals.

B:2 Kjerulf *Cradle Song*

Don't let your pupil be put off by the blackness of the page or complexity of the key signature, or they could miss out on one of the most charming and beautiful pieces in the list. This choice will, undoubtedly, need a fairly assured pianist, with a technical competence that provides the freedom to control the balance and colour. Begin by insisting that pupils are fluent in F sharp major and E flat minor scales and arpeggios, so that their fingers have a physical instinct for the shapes and patterns of these keys. Thereafter, it is a matter of lots of slow-motion musical practice, listening and adjusting, deciding what is important as far as the melodic line is concerned, and keeping everything else out of the way. The right hand will, out of necessity, have to jump from position to position in the opening, but this should be done in a controlled way so that a sense of line is maintained.

Notice that the A♯ at the beginning of bar 3 is part of the melody that is continued by the left hand and then given back in bar 4. The accent in bars 9, 10, 13 and 14 should be interpreted expressively, not aggressively, and the wonderful tenor tune in bars 21–24 should come as no surprise to the performer – let this be a magical and transporting moment for the listener.

The middle section could easily wake up any sleeping child: the octaves and compass of the keyboard may encourage a rather boisterous tone. In fact, just as much subtlety of nuance and balance is needed as in the more obviously gentle opening. Rather than increase the tempo here, take as much time as is needed, perhaps using *una corda* for at least one of the *pianissimo* phrases.

Achieving a gentle tone in the right-hand octaves requires a soft 'drop' on to the keys, lifting between each octave during the very soft accompanying chords, and grading the line intuitively. The pedal will almost certainly need to change on the first, third and fourth quaver beats of the bar.

Pupils will need to appreciate the wonder and delight of the harmonic changes, particularly in bars 41 and 45. Time taken over these will entrance the listener, whereas if played in strict time, they sound totally insensitive.

91

Bar 47 is quite a stretch, and will need plenty of time, musically and technically. The ending will require a delicate touch, a true *ppp*, with the necessary holding of the pedal through the final two bars. This is to produce a colourful and velvety cushion of sound, through which the memory of the melody can delicately send the child to sleep.

B:3 Lyadov *Mazurka in F minor*

The more tortured souls among your pupils may well find this piece therapeutic, being so full of mournful Romantic chromaticism and anguished, spacious intervals. The mazurka character takes a back seat to the expressive nature of the piece, although the rhythms continually allude to the dance.

F minor may not be such a familiar key to pupils, so use this piece as an opportunity to consolidate the scale and arpeggio, whether the pupil has chosen Group 2 or not. The more fluent pupils are with the geography and patterns of this key, the more comfortably the piece will sit under the fingers.

Technically, the demands are not really posed by the notes but by the sound world, balance and natural rubato that the piece requires. In the opening, the melody should be uninterrupted by the left-hand harmonies, which should stay right out of the way. This is particularly important underneath the decaying first C, and where the textures become thicker, such as in bars 7–8. All harmony notes (the B♭ in bar 3 and most minims elsewhere) should be held conscientiously with the fingers, to allow some freedom for pedal changes.

The tearful *poco più mosso* should not become boisterous or too loud, and it is vital to the character that the semiquavers are kept tucked in and not played as triplets. The melody is still at the top here, and there is no need to try to bring out the imitative middle texture: it will be heard anyway, so better to insist on a softer pianistic colour.

An appropriate use of rubato will greatly enhance the performance, in particular through the quavers (in bars 3–5, for instance), where a gentle accelerando and then stretching of the pulse will help bring expressive purpose to the irregular phrase lengths. Pupils should also understand the overall structure and perhaps take time easing their way into new sections.

It is impossible to dictate the pedalling, which will very much depend on the instrument and room. Accustom pupils to listening to rests and harmonies, to ensure neither is obscured by the pedal. Less pedal rather than more will be needed in the *poco più mosso* section, and bass harmonies should be held with the finger where possible.

Insist that a pupil holds the final chord for its full length (plus a pause), and retains the atmosphere through the lift of the hands and pedal – a nonchalant ending destroys so many effective performances. Here, it should be bittersweet and sad.

B:4 Glière *Sketch in D sharp minor*

This is a lovely piece with a frightening key signature and lots of accidentals. The best introduction would be to play the piece to your pupils, without letting them see the music. Once a pupil is in sympathy with the mood and style, the incentive to master the notes is far stronger. This means, of course, that you will need to learn the piece, but the effort will be more than worthwhile as you will have experienced exactly what your pupil is hoping to master.

The physical reality of playing the notes is far easier than it looks on the page. Short sections learnt thoroughly will soon result in the whole piece being under the fingers. Some corners will need memorizing, and strong finger memory, as well as a strong aural memory for the melody, will help both practice and performance.

Through all the quavers, aim for a seamless legato, which can only be achieved with systematic fingering. Those who resort to all-too-common improvisation in this respect should be firmly guided towards workable decisions. As D sharp minor is a less familiar key, watch out for misreadings – another reason why learning this piece yourself is an advantage.

The title 'Sketch' is significant. This is not a lavish oil painting, and even the louder passages have a delicate texture, so the tone must always be appealing and not too emphatic.

It's difficult to teach rubato, although the general principles can be explained. This Romantic style of playing depends on the gentle but positive forward flow of phrases towards the main point, which can then be given time to be enjoyed. Playing this style of music strictly in time would take the life out of it.

Pedalling is carefully marked, and following it will avoid smudging the frequent chromaticisms. The quality of tone is central. A beautiful cantabile that emphasizes the dotted crotchets in the right hand (held for their full length) should be the aim. The little hairpins support the melody and often give gentle emphasis to the second beat of the bar. The semi-detached articulation of the left hand in bars 23–24 is an interesting detail, leading to a linking *sotto voce* line before the theme returns at bar 27. This time the theme is warmer in tone because it's an octave lower. There are two instances of *forte*: at bar 21, where it should be given some space (a short allargando will help), and in the very last phrase, where the dynamic should fade quickly, with a small ritardando.

B:5 Il'insky *Berceuse*

Many lullabies appear in the syllabuses, and not only for piano. Some young children, who may or may not understand the meaning of the word 'berceuse', announce that they are about to play 'Berkyoos'. The pronunciation is not important, but the mood certainly is – the ideal being a gentle hypnotic rhythm and a soothing melody.

The technical demands are focused on two necessities: a warm, well-sustained harmonic background in the bass (quite a flat hand will help this, plus, of course, legato pedal), and a beautifully phrased cantabile right-hand melody. This could be the right opportunity to point out that a left-hand accompaniment involves more than just keeping at a lower dynamic than the melody. It also, in really musical performances, complements the movement of the melody, both the forward flow and the slackening, just as an accompanist moulds the music to an independent solo line. Examiners will be alert to this musically sophisticated skill, and sensitive pupils will delight in finding another form of expression.

The first page is all within a *piano* dynamic, but the little crescendos and diminuendos avoid a monotonous sound. Try to find a different kind of *piano* colour at bar 15, where the melody takes a different turn. Throughout the piece, even with pedal the bottom line of minims needs to be firm, held with the fingers whenever possible. Some split 10ths, and arpeggiated chords (one is marked in bar 10), are very much in the style of the piece.

Bars 19–22 are the most sonorous, with the bass E♭ needing a really good tone to survive the ties and changes of pedal. Even if the sound dies away during the second bar, the listener will still 'hear' this note, providing the initial attack is warm enough.

It's interesting to notice that the rallantando starts at the end of bar 21, while the last groups of quavers in bar 22 lead us back to the tempo of the main theme.

The final section is marked *piano*, but bars 31–32 could come up to *mezzo-piano* in order to make the final diminuendo a realistic possibility.

It can be so upsetting in an exam if notes fail to speak due to unfamiliarity with the instrument. Firm fingers at all times will help to prevent these accidents. Hopefully, candidates will take plenty of time over the last two bars and end with a gentle, luxurious arpeggio, which can still be enjoyed through the pause.

B:6 K. Leighton *Andante sostenuto*

This is a sensuous, warm and quite beautiful movement from a wonderful sonatina, and it is a magical choice for the musical pianist – particularly one possessing a natural sense of rubato, good cantabile tone and an instinctive awareness of where to pedal. Large hands are a bonus, but are not essential.

The tempo must allow the melody a sense of direction, and enable a performer to take time around the corners without stopping the natural flow – so it must not be too slow. The left-hand chords should be velvety soft, and need a gentle, relaxed weight into the keys, with lots of 'give' in the wrist and hand. Where the chords are not stretchable, a very gentle arpeggio is in order, although make sure that the pedal catches the bass note and that any hint of an accent at the top of the chord is avoided at all costs. The pedalling, in general, is fairly obvious, and must support the harmonies, whether chords or arpeggio figures. Let the ear be the judge, as pedalling can be dictated by the melody (in the opening, for example) or by the underlying harmonies.

A sensitive pupil will find it hard not to savour the more expressive moments, and pupils should take time to explore the subtle nuances. They might linger just a little over the first B, or move lightly, yet in time, towards the A. They might ask themselves questions such as: how might the first two smaller phrases be contrasted with the third longer phrase?; how could the first three phrases be made to feel like one long phrase?; or, to what extent should the triplet (in bar 5 and elsewhere) be stretched for expressive effect?

The middle section promises a comforting and optimistic look into the future, and shouldn't be too *più mosso*, particularly as the left-hand quaver movement gives this impression anyway. It needs an improvisatory feel, and certain moments have to be carefully handled, most significantly the arresting key change in bar 29, which can so easily sound like a misreading if not eased in with some sensitivity.

The tone around bar 37 could become quite intense as the register gets higher, so the dynamic will need to be carefully considered.

Pupils should allow a spacious sweep in the left hand three lines from the end, and enjoy the more gentle and caring caress of the final bars.

C:1 C. Lambert *Elegiac Blues*

This slinky and seductive blues is bound to be very popular with young and old alike. A relaxed swing groove is needed throughout, with an instinct for the 'push' behind the third note of the triplet.

The suggested tempo is excellent, but do allow it some breadth within the crotchet = *c*.88. A decisive pulse must be established before beginning, so encourage all pupils to count themselves in; at bar 3 there should be no perceivable change or adjustment to the tempo.

An improvisatory feel is essential to the piece. No small change of personality in the music should sound as though it has taken the performer by surprise. The listener must feel comfortable being led from the cheekier opening and similar moments (such as at bars 13–14) until the smoochy and slightly drunk chromaticism (bars 4–7 etc.). Elsewhere, the blues-like melodies need a comfortable rhythmic change from semiquavers to swung quavers.

Conveniently, the composer has suggested a slight arpeggiation to the left-hand chords. This will help pupils with smaller hands, although careful listening is crucial so that they catch the bass note with the pedal and don't leave the harmonies starved of support. If there is a problem with this, place the bottom note on the beat.

The use of pedalling ranges from subtly enhancing the phrasing to colouring the whole bar. Dabs of pedal – short, on the quaver – will warm up the opening chords, while still showing the rests. The third bar can be pedalled through the first three beats and changed on the fourth, while bar 4 can be pedalled right through, leaving a change until bar 5. In bar 9 keep the pedal at bay until the staccato right-hand chord has come off, and in bar 14 follow the phrasing. Most importantly, experiment with the possibilities.

Textures can easily become thick and mushy, so carefully balance all lines and chords, in particular in the wonderful tenor melodies. Lots of rubato is good, but it must be against a clear pulse. If you can't follow the rhythm, then the pupil is taking too much of a liberty.

Allow plenty of time for the piece to settle into the hands so that it can be performed 'from memory with the music'. Right to the very end, explore and encourage the broadest range of musical colour and dynamic. The listener's mind should be transported to sleazy gangster movies and smoke-filled, whisky-fumed rooms.

C:2 Anthony Payne *Micro-Sonata*

A terrific, vibrant and rewarding piece, *Micro-Sonata* is an excellent addition to any pupil's repertoire. It relies for its energy on scampering semiquaver figures (like wild animals darting in and out of shadows or hedges), imaginative and surprising rhythms, and contrasted dynamics. It is not all fast, however. The *sostenuto e cantabile* section provides a chance to get one's breath back, although the inner chords still keep the heart pumping with nervous energy.

Micro-Sonata, naturally, is short. The note learning may seem slow going at first, but once the rhythmic patterns and fingering are mastered, this piece soon begins to feel comfortable. Pupils will find it so much easier to play if they prepare, carefully, away from the piano: clapping the rhythms, singing the articulation (maybe just on one note), working at rhythmic co-ordination by tapping the rhythms on their knees, and so on. Conduct it through in four so that a feel for the syncopation, changes of mood and the final rallentando to *più lento* is instilled. The actual notes are easier to play if there is already an aural and physical impression within which to work.

The semiquavers require good technical control, as they should be even and have convincing character and dynamic shape. They also need a bright, buoyant tone, with flair and clarity, and too much weight behind the fingers will hinder their movement. Encourage pupils to work at small phrases from memory, listening attentively to the musical shape and the evenness, and looking at the hands to help them understand the patterns and technique needed to achieve certain sounds. Very little pedal is needed, except to enhance the phrasing or to add warmth to some of the lovely chords.

This may not be the most immediately appealing of the List C pieces, but it is worth promoting. If you don't want to learn it yourself, then at least try to give some impression of it and put on your salesman's hat. For a pupil with good, reliable and quick fingers, this piece is a gift!

C:3 Prokofiev *Allegretto*

There are many gems among Prokofiev's 'fleeting visions', and this is one of them. It is really worth exploring this collection, and perhaps you could get your pupils to play through a few of the less texturally complex pieces. Even if they play only the first two bars, your pupils will have got a taste of the different characters, not to mention having had some sight-reading practice!

Visions fugitives, then, is a collection of images, vividly remembered but reflecting a moment in time. This one yearns for something – it is anxious at first, but with a rather sarcastic humour in the middle section.

This Allegretto is not a fast piece. It does not respond well to too much rhythmic rigidity, especially in the first page, so a little ebb and flow is needed – as well as time given at the ends of phrases.

Rather as in his Prelude in C major, Prokofiev contrasts the legato outer sections of this piece with something much more detached in nature and possessing rhythmic individuality.

Technically, there are some challenges, particularly for small hands. The left hand will require some slow and musical practice, with and without pedal, to convey an easy sense of line and musical shape. In bars 5 and 6 the bottom notes must be held with the finger, as the pedal is likely to change on the third beat. In bars 7, 8 and 9 the pedal should catch the bass notes, so pupils will have to get used to the co-ordination between foot and hand here.

The middle section requires almost no pedal at all. Here the problems relate to achieving a fluent, controlled yet characterful right hand. The semiquavers demand a virtuosity and sparkle, with the phrasing clearly articulated. The accented notes need to be carefully placed, while the interrupting C♯ in bar 16 should be clearly highlighted. Keep the left-hand major 2nds held – across each other – with the fingers.

In bar 26 the left hand may look impossible. If distributed between the hands as marked, the A♮ can continue the line and the left-hand bottom D can be brought in with this note, continuing with a quick light arpeggio chord to give plenty of time to arrive at the left-hand B. The inner line here, and at the beginning, should be clearly defined, with no sense of thick texture – just a melody through warm yet gentle harmonies.

The piece will suit pupils with very good listening skills, as they will need to be continually alert to the sound world they are producing in performance. Encourage musical thinking and listening beyond the notes, right up to the final bar and the melancholy shift to D minor – a musical tear rolling down the cheek.

C:4 Bartók *Bagpipers*

There is a festive feel to this movement of Bartók's excellent *Sonatina*. The bold drone in the left hand and quick graces are part of bagpipe music everywhere, and not just in Scotland – the bagpipe (in various forms) is found in musical culture throughout the world, most notably, as here, in folk music. After the grand introduction, the games commence, with all the fun of the fair and a village dance, drama or spectacle. The event is then 'piped out' in style.

It would be dishonest to say that this is an easy movement to play: the left hand in particular needs a certain confidence and ease of movement around the keyboard. The jumps from the middle-register chords to the bass notes are quick, and will have to be made without looking. The better the right hand is known, and the more independent it is, then the easier it will be to have a glance at the left hand. For this reason, encourage your pupils to learn the melody from memory. This will also give them opportunity to explore the musical personality within the *forte* dynamic, while gaining fluency in the rhythms. Observe the details of articulation and discuss how these could be interpreted, especially the tenuto marks. The pedalling may seem generous, but it works very well, providing a clear tone is maintained in the right hand and the left hand is kept suitably out of its way. All sforzando 5ths must be caught with the pedal.

The middle section makes its own demands on the performer, but these mostly concern the rhythm, articulation and phrasing. The articulation should be clearly defined and buoyant, while the changes of time signature, from 2/4 to 3/4 and back, should be felt as well as counted.

The leggiero touch and clarity is generally achieved from the surface of the key, with active fingers and just a little lift before phrases that start with an emphasis. There is nothing harsh in the sound world here, and heavy-footed tone should be avoided.

The ritardando at the end of this section, and the return to the opening tempo, represents a wonderful moment, when the frivolities fade into the distance and the bagpiper reappears from around the corner.

A convincing performance will require a technical and musical confidence and self-belief, as well as effective control of the middle section, but it is a terrific piece and one for the natural show-offs.

C:5 Pēteris Plakidis *Distant Song*

As is so often the case, rhythmically complex and less traditionally notated compositions often look complicated on paper. In fact, this atmospheric and enormously effective piece is not at all hard to play, after some careful reading, initial counting and sorting out.

Make a point of reading the footnote to this piece before deciding upon the pedalling. Use pedal to warm up the opening chords, or simple legato pedalling wherever the right hand has rests. But use none at all during the right-hand outbursts as, particularly in bar 2 (final chord), the melody itself draws out a resonance from the left-hand chord. Try playing this chord silently, holding it down and then playing the demisemiquavers. A bit more pedal might be used in bar 5 and through the first dotted-crotchet beat of bar 6, but elsewhere add dabs where it doesn't interfere.

To achieve the *acutao* in the opening, use a firm bounce with active fingers in the right hand, but then grade all the dynamics down from this until the sad song enters at bar 5. The grief-stricken initial outbursts eventually die down to gentle sobs, and there is a glimpse of happier times in bar 7 before the air of melancholy returns. Here, there might be just a hint of 'pulling oneself together'.

The description *quasi coro* for the left-hand chords is very helpful. These should be balanced and unobtrusive, but have enough tone to last for the appropriate length. The dynamic range is extremely wide, and should be clearly defined throughout, from the softest *ppp* to the most intense *fff*. Ask the pupil to play from the beginning of the piece, and imagine that you are writing in the dynamics you hear. Then see if they match those in the score. Better still, record your pupil's playing, and let him or her be the judge.

If the expressive detail is observed and interpreted within this context, all other concerns are rhythmic. Do plenty of work with the pupil away from the piano, so that the rhythms can be internalized without the added burden of right and wrong notes. Conduct phrases through together and clap them as duets, or perhaps tap the pulse and then play them in scalic figures, until they can be 'felt'.

In the end, don't just rely on the detail but add that sense of inventiveness, atmosphere and imagery that distinguishes the distinction performance.

C:6 Shostakovich *Prelude in E flat minor*

If your pupil loves dark sonorities and has the character to cope with the most foreboding of scenarios, then this is the piece for him or her. A big rich sound is required, and larger hands may help this, but otherwise there are few technical demands. A successful performance, then, will rely on an unflinching pulse; careful judgement of dynamic; and plenty of tone, particularly at the climax of the piece.

The opening perhaps gives an impression of the huge machinery of war moving slowly but inevitably over a vast inhospitable landscape. Demonstrate the different ways of balancing the chords and melodic motif in the opening bars, and invite your pupils to adopt the sound they think best draws out the drama and imagery. Elsewhere it will be crucial to explore a vivid range of piano timbre. An equal tone on both notes in the left-hand octaves works well, but 'voicing' the octaves to the top in bar 13 will be even more effective – a glimpse of heaven soon interrupted by the menacing B♭s.

The triplet B♭s from bar 15 onwards should be kept a little out of the way. Once the string is vibrating, it only needs a bit of extra impetus to build up the tone, and there is a long way to go – right up to the *fff* in bar 24. This should be maintained for the next four bars, with the support of the left-hand octaves and the benefit of extremes of register. Thereafter the texture begins to thin out, slightly anticipating the diminuendo. Don't be too fussy or obsessed with bar 24. This is a passionate gesture, and as long as the chords on the first and third beats are together, then the quintuplet semi-quavers are simply stretched between them.

One of the common problems in a performance of this prelude will be the quality of the *fff* tone. Examiners have difficulty putting politely into words that passages were ugly and too forceful in sound. No pianist can deny, though, just how disturbing an inappropriate percussiveness can be, so make sure pupils use their natural shock absorber (the wrist) to avoid this. The marked pedalling does work, particularly on an upright piano, but it is a touch too generous on a grand, so change more often if the sound becomes too muddy and confused.

Check the notes carefully; it is easy to miss a flat or two. Ensure the final dotted minims are held for their full value, slowly lifting the notes just before the pedal to convey the rather depressing and soulful end.